MOSCOW

C000183562

TARIQ ALI

Born and educated in Pakistan and subsequently at Oxford
University, Tariq Ali is a writer and film-maker who was for four
years producer of Channel 4's *Bandung File* and now produces *Rear
Window*. Well known in the 1960s and '70s as an international
political activist, he is the author of over a dozen books on history,
world politics and biography, including *Revolution from Above: Where
is the Soviet Union Going?* His first novel *Redemption* was published in
Autumn 1990. He lives in London.

HOWARD BRENTON

Born in Portsmouth in 1942 and educated at Cambridge University,
Howard Brenton has written well over twenty stage plays as well as
translations, adaptations and screenplays such as his four-part TV
thriller, *Dead Head*. His best-known theatre work is *Christie in Love,
Bloody Poetry, The Churchill Play* (twice revived by the Royal
Shakespeare Company), *Weapons of Happiness, The Romans in Britain*
and *Pravda* (co-written with David Hare) – all three premiered at
the National Theatre – as well as *Iranian Nights*, a response to the
Rushdie affair, co-written with Tariq Ali and premiered at the Royal
Court Theatre. His first novel, *Diving for Pearls*, published in 1989, is
due to be filmed in 1991.

by the same authors

Tariq Ali

Biography

The Nehrus and the Gandhis
Streetfighting Years: An
   Autobiography of the Sixties

History

Revolution from Above: Where is
   the Soviet Union Going?
The Stalinist Legacy (*editor*)
Trotsky for Beginners

World Politics

Can Pakistan Survive?
Who's Afraid of Margaret
   Thatcher? (*with Ken
   Livingstone*)

Novel

Redemption

TV Plays

Partition
Liberty's Scream

Howard Brenton

Plays

Bloody Poetry
The Churchill Play
Epsom Downs
The Genius
Greenland
H.I.D. (Hess is Dead)
Hitler Dances
Magnificence
Revenge
The Romans in Britain
Sore Throats
Thirteenth Night
Weapons of Happiness

Screenplay

Dead Head

Collections

Plays: One
Plays: Two
Plays for the Poor Theatre

Collaborations

Brassneck (*with David Hare*)
Pravda (*with David Hare*)
A Short Sharp Shock
   (*with Tony Howard*)
Sleeping Policemen
   (*with Tunde Ikoli*)

Translations

Bertolt Brecht's Life of Galileo
Georg Büchner's Danton's
   Death

Tariq Ali and Howard Brenton

Iranian Nights

Novel

Diving for Pearls

TARIQ ALI and HOWARD BRENTON

MOSCOW GOLD

NICK HERN BOOKS

A division of Walker Books Limited

A Nick Hern Book

Moscow Gold first published in 1990 as an original paperback by
Nick Hern Books, a division of Walker Books Limited, 87 Vauxhall
Walk, London SE11 5HJ

Moscow Gold copyright © 1990 Tariq Ali and Howard Brenton
Introduction: *An Explanatory Note*
copyright © 1990 Tariq Ali and Howard Brenton
Appendices
1: *Gold in Moscow* copyright © 1990 Howard Brenton
2: *How Can We Do It, Vsevolod?* copyright © 1990 Howard Brenton
3: *Excerpts from a Diary* copyright © 1990 by Tariq Ali
4: *From the Dictatorship of Weakness to a Democracy of Strength*
copyright © 1988 Tariq Ali

Front cover picture by Stasys Eidrigevičius

Set in ITC New Baskerville and printed in Great Britain by
Expression Printers Ltd, London N7 9DP

British Library Cataloguing in Publication Data

Brenton, Howard 1942-
    Moscow gold.
    I. Title   II. Tariq Ali 1943-
    822.914

ISBN 1 85459 078 2

Caution
All rights whatsoever in this play are strictly reserved. Requests to
reproduce the text in whole or in part should be addressed to the
publisher. Application for performance in any medium or for
translation into any language should be made to Margaret Ramsay
Limited, 14a Goodwin's Court, St Martin's Lane, London WC2 4LL.

This book is sold subject to the condition that it shall not, by way of
trade or otherwise, be lent, resold, hired out, or otherwise circulated
without the publisher's consent in any form of binding or cover
other than that in which it is published and without a similar
condition including this condition being imposed on the
subsequent purchaser.

In memory of John Dexter

An Explanatory Note

Moscow Gold was born in May 1989 in a dingy dressing room of the
Royal Court Theatre on the day we finished writing the last page of
Iranian Nights, a one-act intervention into the cultural crisis known
as the 'Rushdie affair'. The collaboration had gone well, but it had
finished too quickly. We sat talking about the state of the world and
it soon became clear that what excited us was the Soviet Union. It
was not impressionistic chatter. That would not have been enough
to embark on a new collective enterprise. Why not a play? Put them
all on the stage! We roared with laughter at the absurdity of such a
notion and the idea was temporarily shelved as we were submerged
in the rehearsals of *Iranian Nights* and subsequently became
somewhat preoccupied by the hysteria which surrounded the
opening of that forty-five minute production.

Two unrelated events revived our interest rapidly. A BBC friend
conveyed a congratulatory message from Arthur Miller who had
enjoyed *Iranian Nights*. 'This is what the theatre should be about!'

Some days later John Dexter came to see the play, liked and it
and invited us to lunch. We told him about *Moscow Gold*. He became
very excited. 'Go away and write it', was his advice. 'When you've
finished it I'll tell you if it's crap.' We did. Eight months later we
presented John Dexter with the play. He enjoyed it immensely and
began to work on it immediately. The play was accepted by the RSC.
Then John Dexter became ill. He worked from his hospital bed
where we were summoned regularly. Sadly, John never recovered.
His death was unexpected. We had been working on it so closely
with him that his absence left a vacuum, a pain and a deep
depression. Hence the dedication – a tiny posthumous tribute from
two writers who miss him greatly.

The RSC was determined to stage the play this autumn and,
fortunately, there was no argument as to the director. Barry Kyle
took over the project. His enthusiasm for the play and his
remarkable energy revitalised us as well. We began again and were
delighted when Stefanos Lazaridis agreed to design the set. We
were, frankly, stunned when Stefanos took us through the play with
his model of the design. We felt that our play had finally been
liberated!

Moscow Gold is a song of history as it *is*, not as it should be and,
apart from one utopian lapse, not as we would like it to be. It is a
chronicle of sorrow and anger, pain and despair, high hope and
high anxiety, frustration and fatalism as experienced by all Soviet
citizens in Moscow, that metropolis of the world where history

confronts us in every corner. The French lyric-poet Baudelaire, in the course of an essay titled 'Progress' paused to tell his readers a story, which for him was the essence of criticism:

> The story is told of M. Balzac (and who would not listen with respect to any anecdote, no matter how trivial, concerning that great genius?) that one day he found himself in front of a beautiful picture – a melancholy winter-scene, heavy with hoarfrost and thinly sprinkled with cottages and mean-looking peasants; and that after gazing at a little house from which a thin wisp of smoke was rising, 'How beautiful is is!', he cried. 'But what are they doing in that cottage? What are their thoughts? What are their sorrows? Has it been a good harvest? No doubt they have bills to pay?'

That speaks for what we felt writing our play: the political struggle is spectacular, of fire and ice, and great to dramatise; but no doubt they need food to eat, they need to be given a choice of clothes, of shoes; no doubt they need toothpaste to clean their teeth; they need syringes in hospitals which cure infections rather than injecting them . . . Without understanding the deprivations which the citizens of the Soviet Union have undergone since the thirties, it is impossible to understand the changes which are taking place. The cancer might have been stopped without a surgeon's knife in 1956 with the Khrushchev thaw or in 1968, with the Prague spring, but today a major operation is necessary. A transplanted 'free' market may only provide temporary respite, but it seems better to many than a descent to sure death. The idea is, understandably, anathema to many socialists and liberals in the West. John Kenneth Galbraith recently warned the Soviet people not to put any blind trust in a market which had so patently failed to deliver the goods in the United States. But this moderate appeal from a distinguished American Democrat, one of many, went unheeded!

Moscow Gold laughs and cries, but, above all, it tries to understand the very real human needs of the Soviet people as well as the dilemmas which confront the Soviet leader Mikhail Gorbachev. Under the pressure of events which they themselves have unleashed, political leaders, too, undergo a change. Boris Yeltsin starts off his career championing 'social justice' and when the play ends he is an ardent 'free marketeer'. Gorbachev, too, is moving in that direction. 'It's not easy', we have him saying to Raisa in the play, 'making history under circumstances which are out of our control.' The people on their part become more and more desperate and nationalism, that logic of perverse unreason, finally begins to reach a demented level. Imagined utopias are projected onto the past and then recycled as visions of the future.

Moscow Gold tries to explain the present rather than develop a particular set of theses. In that sense it owes much more to the work of Meyerhold (see pp.90-92) than to Brecht. The choice was deliberate. The changes in the East have transformed world politics. Uncertainty has replaced the tried and tested formulas of both Right and Left. The nettle we had to grasp, as socialist writers, was that there are no longer easy ideological solutions. What we are witnessing is an epochal change which will shape politics for three, four or five generations. This involves a rethink for everyone: cold warriors as well as closet Brezhnevites, not to mention those on both extremes of the spectrum who can treat the upheavals either as an irreversible capitalist triumph or a fantastical betrayal of the socialist cause by Mikhail Gorbachev and his friends. Both views are wrong. A simpleton's view of history.

It is the very fluidity of the newly-emerging world order which will throw up new movements. The new Polish régime, to take but one instance, has made Catholic education compulsory in their country. Tomorrow they will outlaw abortion. For us it is impossible to conceive that such obvious regressions will be accepted tamely for an indefinite period. To use a capitalist cliché, 'the world is up for grabs'; to use a socialist cliché, 'the world is ours to remake.'

It has taken us a year to finish this play. A year in which watching the news bulletins was often an intensely subjective experience. But we kept our nerve by refusing to accept the punditry of the western media which had Gorbachev on the ropes every three months. We structured the play in such a fashion that, barring unforeseen tragedies, the opening and the end were permanent fixtures. We allowed ourselves the luxury of two scenes which we could change till the very last moment and we hope that the version you read on these pages is the final one, but if it is not we crave your indulgence. It is impossible to compete with history.

Tariq Ali   Howard Brenton
12 August 1990

Moscow Gold was first performed by the Royal Shakespeare Company at the Barbican Theatre, London on 20 September 1990. Press night was 26 September. The cast was as follows:

MIKHAIL GORBACHEV	David Calder
RAISA GORBACHEV	Sara Kestelman
BORIS YELTSIN	Russell Dixon
YEGOR LIGACHEV	Frank Moorey
ALEXANDER YAKOVLEV	Robert Putt
ANDREI GROMYKO/SOVIET MINER	John Drake
MARSHAL USTINOV	Michael Hughes
RIMMA ZHUKOVA	Penny Ryder
GRISHIN/RYZHKOV/EGON KRENZ	William Chubb
ERICH HONECKER	Frank Mills
NIKOLAI CEAUȘESCU/RASHIDOV	Richard Earthy
ELEANOR CEAUȘESCU	Sara Llewellyn
VICTOR, ex-editor of *Pravda*	Marcus Eyre
YURI ANDROPOV	Clifford Rose
LENIN	Clive Merrison
CHERNOBYL MAN/GENERAL GROMOV	John Kane
ZOYA	Paola Dionisotti
LENA ⎫ Three Kremlin cleaners	Darlene Johnson
KATYA ⎭	Gabrielle Lloyd
GRIGORI (GRISHA), a KGB veteran, married to ZOYA	Joseph O'Conor
YOUNG BORIS, ZOYA and GRIGORI's son	Mark Williams
LARISSA, betrothed to YOUNG BORIS	Abigail Thaw
RONA ANDERSON, an astrologer/ SHEVARDNADZE	Craig Pinder
STALINIST CHEMISTRY TEACHER	Judith Brydon
ARMENIAN EARTHQUAKE VICTIM/ KIRLENKO	Peter Bygott
PEPSI VENDOR/LENINGRAD PUNK	Simon D'Arcy
FLYING TYPIST	Matthew Warman
WAITER IN CO-OP RESTAURANT/ LENINGRAD PUNK	Richard Doubleday
MOSCOW GANGSTER	Jason Flemyng
BALTIC FOLKLORIST/BALLERINA	Natalie Roles

The cast play many other parts, including: sailors and revolutionaries in 1917, Politburo members, people in the Moscow queues, Moscow gangsters, Soviet miners, Baltic folklorists, a Leningrad rock band, security men, Moscow Mafia gangsters, Muslims from the South, travellers at Moscow Airport.

Directed by Barry Kyle
Designed by Stefanos Lazaridis
Lighting Designer Alan Burrett
Music by Bill Connor
Choreography by Beyhan
Assistant Director Alan McCormack
Stage Manager Eric Lumsden
Deputy Stage Manager Neil Constable
Assistant Stage Manager Ian Morgan James
Assistant Stage Manager Liz Griffiths

ACT ONE: Before the Wall

Scene One

A huge oval table. Its vast surface is empty.
At the head of the table, centre stage, sits V.I. LENIN. *His fist is raised,*
clenched.
A silence.
Then his fist falls to the table to a loud drumbeat. He stands. He speaks
quietly.

LENIN. We will now proceed to construct the socialist order.

Huge traps in the centre of the table fly open. A Festival of the Oppressed
erupts everywhere. It is the Russian Revolution. A banner gives the year,
1917. Music – strains of the Internationale and the Marseillaise
overpowered by the music of the play – and drumbeats mix with shots fired
in the air. SAILORS *are carrying giant red flags. The Tsarist flag is torn*
and replaced with the hammer and sickle. Men and women WORKERS
with banners and posters of Lenin and Trotsky. MAYAKOVSKY *is*
declaiming. Three women are caught up in the swirling scene, ZOYA,
KATYA *and* LENA. KATYA, *with a group of young friends, carrying*
placards – constructivist and other avant-garde paintings. The pageant is
like a volcano in constant flow. Its elements are: a participatory dance in
which LENIN *is active, of political and alcoholic intoxication – there is*
the flaunting of wine bottles from the cellars of the nobility – which are
depleted within a month – the proletariat drunk on the finest French
wines. LENIN *establishes some order in the chaotic dance as* TROTSKY
consigns the enemies of the Revolution to the dustbin of history. It ends
with LENIN *carried on the* SAILORS' *shoulders and a rendering of the*
Internationale. Then a Meyerholdian pyramid with LENIN *on the top as*
all noise and action stops. The tableau is motionless, as if for a still
photograph. Lights flash off and on with the noise of a camera shutter.
Then music starts up again, a funeral dirge with the SAILORS *carrying*
LENIN *as if he were a coffin down with them. A typist sitting at an 'old-*
fashioned' typewriter flies above the scene. Reams of paper come from his
machine.

KATYA *and* LENA *move forward and begin to clothe and age* ZOYA. *A banner gives the year, 1982.*

ZOYA. How am I what I am? What did I come from? The years of hopes and fears. Civil war. Famine. The Terror. Hitler. The lost millions, are they my family? Oh! The stark little sentence, the stark little phrase, 'the Soviet Union lost millions' . . . Does that mean my life? And now all that's left . . . is the mess, and we clean it up every day. Under Brezhnev we have become detached, living according to our own sad and lonely laws. I can't think about the present. The past is bright for me, despite all its sufferings, and sometimes the future, but the present is hazy. The only ones who enjoy the present are the gang who sit around this table.

LENA. Politburo meetings. Not like the old days.

KATYA. Remember in Comrade Stalin's time when there really was some shit to clear up?

ZOYA. Marshal Vorisholov!

LENA *and* KATYA *laugh.*

KATYA. Vorisholov! Remember that day he got so scared when Molotov was under attack that he messed his pants?

ZOYA. Stalin insisted they all carry a second pair!

The THREE WOMEN *clean the table with huge mops and brooms. The Politburo of 1982 assembles, a group of fourteen men, most of them looking old and sick, smiles frozen upon their faces. Great deference is made to* CHERNENKO *who walks on, aided on one side by* GROMYKO *and on the other by the sinister looking* GRISHIN – *boss of the Moscow Party. Following them is* RASHIDOV, *the Party boss of Uzbekistan. He is a Uriah Heap figure, exuding self-effacement. Also* MARSHAL USTINOV, *huge-bellied and stiff-backed, in a uniform encrusted with medals.*
Two men, wearing regular Politburo suits, keep apart from the old men. They are YURI V. ANDROPOV *and* MIKHAIL SERGEYEVICH GORBACHEV. GORBACHEV *is, by far, the youngest man present.*

CHERNENKO. Did Reagan really say that?

GROMYKO. Yes I heard him.

CHERNENKO, GROMYKO *and* GRISHIN *roar with laughter.*

CHERNENKO (*affectionately*). Comrade Grishin. Where did you get your car telephone?

GRISHIN *grins, sheepishly.*

GRISHIN. It was a gift.

GROMYKO. I know. We all know.

GORBACHEV (*to* ANDROPOV). What is this emergency meeting about?

ANDROPOV. All meetings of the Politburo are emergency meetings. They have one function. Not to let anything emerge.

GORBACHEV *makes an impatient gesture.* ANDROPOV *pats him on the back, gently.*

Patience, Mikhail Sergeyevich, patience. Try and look happy.

CHERNENKO. Comrades! Let . . .

His voice is high pitched and shaky when he speaks publicly. They all look at him.

Let . . .

A pause.

Let's start.

A VOICE (*shocked*). Without Comrade Brezhnev?

CHERNENKO. He will come along later. You have the agenda before you. As you know Comrade Rashidov is here specially to report on agriculture in Uzbekistan.

GORBACHEV (*to* ANDROPOV). This will take four fucking hours.

ANDROPOV *smiles.* RASHIDOV *puffs himself up. He takes out a thick wad of a hundred page document from his briefcase. He drones self-importantly into his speech.*

RASHIDOV. Comrades. I am honoured to be invited to a Politburo meeting. The last occasion I was honoured was when you decided to send our troops into Afghanistan. We were proud to fight under the Soviet flag.

Uneasy looks between USTINOV *and* GROMYKO. RASHIDOV *notices immediately. He discards three of the pages.*

Under comrade Brezhnev's wise and inspired leadership our region has prospered. Comrades! We have fulfilled all our targets. In 1972, exactly a decade ago, cotton production was stagnating.

GORBACHEV *leans his head back and looks up at the ceiling. He speaks his thoughts.* RASHIDOV *continues to mouth his boring speech.*

GORBACHEV. Stalin called the cotton 'white gold'. So, to clothe the Soviet masses, plough up an entire republic! Grow one crop! Thousands of square kilometres, let the people's white gold stretch horizon to horizon! Result? A monoculture. Farms levelled. The soil ruined. Cotton dust on the wind, wrecking workers' lungs. What is the reality, a thousand miles from this table in Uzbekistan? Dust, dust, poverty and dust. My country, you are magnificent. You never do anything by halves.

RASHIDOV (*continuing his speech*). Today, thanks to the wise and inspired leadership of our dear Leonid Ilyich, who visited our region several times, cotton production has soared to new heights . . .

The lights go down and at once rise again. The one hundred sheets of RASHIDOV's speech are now spread upon the table. He is reading his last sentence. CHERNENKO is fast asleep.

I pledge that next year production will rise even higher under the wise and inspired leadership of Comrade Brezhnev.

He sits down. The silence wakes up CHERNENKO.

ANDROPOV (*to GORBACHEV*). He is one of the most corrupt men in the party.

GORBACHEV. And stupid! Which is worse?

GRISHIN leans forward on the table.

GRISHIN. A fine report. Comrades, the resolution you have already read. A lot of money is involved here. But I think we are all agreed that it should be granted. I suggest we move straight to the vote. We've discussed this one many times.

A VOICE (*as before*). But where is comrade Brezhnev?

CHERNENKO (*looking at his watch*). I think he'll spare us a moment now.

He gestures off-stage. KATYA, ZOYA and LENA wheel on a coffin at speed. They slide the coffin from its trolley and push it to the centre of the table.

All those in favour of the resolution?

Everyone looks at the coffin. A silence. Then a hand emerges. All hands go up at once. KATYA, LENA and ZOYA hitch up their skirts, leap onto the table and robustly move the coffin back to its trolley and wheel it off.

I think we'll break for lunch.

The members of the Politburo begin to drift off, except for GORBACHEV *and* ANDROPOV.

(*To* GRISHIN.) Is your car phone Sony or Panasonic?

And GORBACHEV *and* ANDROPOV *are alone at the table.* GORBACHEV *is irritated.* ANDROPOV *sits completely still, sphinx-like.*

GORBACHEV. How can you, who know so much, just sit there and listen?

ANDROPOV, *with a flicker of a smile.*

ANDROPOV. The task of the KGB, my dear Mikhail Sergeyevich, is always to listen. But let me ask the same question. Why do you just sit there and listen?

GORBACHEV. It was you who put me here. Can a pupil outshine his master?

ANDROPOV. According to the law of dialectics, if the pupil is any good, he must.

GORBACHEV. According to the same law of dialectics the pupil could end up in the cellars of the KGB!

ANDROPOV. Listen to me, Mikhail Sergeyevich. Have you forgotten where I was in 1956?

A pause.

GORBACHEV. You were our Ambassador in Budapest.

ANDROPOV. Exactly. Hungary 1956, the rising in the streets. I saw it coming. I met them every day. Good, decent, honest Hungarian communists who wanted change. The students worshipped them. The country supported them. What did they want? More freedom. Reality. A real people's democracy. The ghost inside this ugly machine. I met the Hungarian leader Imre Nagy every day. When you hear someone speaking aloud what are your innermost and secret thoughts, it can be both exhilarating and frightening.

GORBACHEV. Didn't you say this to the men around this table?

ANDROPOV. I remember Suslov sitting in that chair, his face frozen like a Siberian winter, telling me: 'Comrade Andropov if we let this disease spread it will not stop there. It will infect the very corpuscles of socialism.' I argued for several hours, but they would not listen. Khrushchev had just denounced Stalin at the Twentieth Party Congress. And the men around this table were scared. I was ordered to crush the rebellion and execute its leaders. Which I did. And you would have done the same in my place!

A pause.

GORBACHEV. Yuri Vladimirovich. You have got to lead this party.

A pause.

ANDROPOV. I know.

The members of the Politburo come back onto the stage, having had lunch. GRISHIN is drunk. Others are the worse for wear. Their conversation is animated. Then they see the two figures sitting together at the table. They fall silent, the smiles wiped from their faces. They resume their seats.

CHERNENKO. Order. Comrade Romanov has the floor.

ROMANOV *looks unsure.*

The report on the new oil pipeline and the talks with the German trade delegation.

ROMANOV *nods and rises. He drains a tumbler of water. Before he can start an* AIDE *rushes in and whispers to* CHERNENKO.
CHERNENKO *begins to tremble as though he is on the verge of a seizure.*

ANDROPOV (*aggressively*). What is going on?

CHERNENKO. Comrade Brezhnev is dead.

A VOICE (*as before*). But he was in the best of health.

The lights go down. The lights go up. ANDROPOV *is sitting in* LENIN*'s chair. The members of the Politburo are still in their seats. The huge table is covered by wreaths.*

ANDROPOV. Comrades, I thank you for electing me General Secretary of the Communist Party of the Soviet Union.

They open their briefcases in business-like fashion. KATYA, LENA *and* ZOYA *come on, clamber up onto the table and begin to remove the wreaths.*

ZOYA. When Stalin died, we all went out into the streets and cried. Come on, own up. We cried our eyes out.

KATYA. Grief?

LENA. Relief!

ZOYA. Not knowing what was coming next. For this one I felt
nothing.

KATYA. My bath taps!

LENA. What do you mean, your bath taps?

KATYA. When we finally moved, we had a bathroom on the landing.
The day Brezhnev died I went to have a bath. Turned the taps on
and sand came out.

ZOYA. I've been having sandy baths for twenty years.

KATYA, *in disbelief.*

KATYA. Even you, Zoya? Surely your Grigori . . .

ZOYA. Even me! Grisha has never registered for special privileges,
nor has he ever let me! And we've been offered them all. The
party schools for the boys, the special clinics, the Swedish
furniture, the cases of French wines . . . We put up with sand
coming out of our bath taps, like everyone else. Grisha, you were
going to say, my Grisha! Sometimes I think my husband must be
the only honest member of the Moscow KGB! And his colleagues
hate his guts for it.

LENA. What about this new one? Cold fish, I've heard.

KATYA. He looks ill.

LENA (*to* ZOYA). Your Grigori knows him, then? At work?

LENA *and* KATYA *look at each other knowingly.*

ZOYA. You know very well my Grisha's worked there for fifty years.
He says this one's different.

KATYA. Will he stop the sand coming out of my bath taps?

*They have picked up the wreaths. They jump down from the table and go
off.*

ANDROPOV. This meeting is over, comrades.

Papers are being put away.

GRISHIN. But comrade . . .

All dead still, watching and listening.

Some of your proposals are too . . . too . . .

ANDROPOV. What?

GRISHIN. Too . . .

ANDROPOV. Too what? Too dangerous? Too radical?

GRISHIN. Not at all comrade!

ANDROPOV. Or too close to your bone?

A silence.

This meeting *is* over.

The members of the Politburo leave, some uneasily. ANDROPOV *gestures to* GORBACHEV *to remain.*
A trap opens in the table, a distraught RASHIDOV, *in pyjamas, steps up onto the table. Three* POLICEMEN *enter.* RASHIDOV *looks from one to the other.*

RASHIDOV. I am still the First Secretary of the Uzbek Party. You have no right to question me.

The POLICEMEN *stare at him.*

I know you're from Moscow. You bastards had better take care. I have powerful friends, on the Politburo.

The POLICEMEN *continue to stare.*

All right I'll answer your questions.

FIRST POLICEMAN. Citizen Rashidov. You used state funds to construct three villas, two in Tashkent and one in the country. Members of your family occupy these at the moment. In one of them we found a cellar full of gold ingots. Can you explain these facts?

SECOND POLICEMAN. You authorised the construction of an underground torture chamber, where your cronies settled private scores. By what legally constituted body of the state was this authorised?

RASHIDOV *begins to disintegrate.*

THIRD POLICEMAN. We know you had protectors in Moscow. A full list of their names will be greatly appreciated. It might help at your trial.

RASHIDOV. What trial?

FIRST POLICEMAN. Citizen Rashidov, since you have not denied any of these charges, we will recommend that the Politburo expels you from the Party in order to permit your trial under the Criminal Code.

The POLICEMAN *go off.* RASHIDOV*'s legs give out, he plumps down upon the table. He unbuttons his pyjama top as if to scratch an armpit, but instead withdraws a revolver from a shoulder holster and shoots himself in the mouth.*
KATYA, LENA *and* ZOYA *rush in,* KATYA *with a large mop. She cleans furiously. They drag the body from the table.*

KATYA. Bloodstains.

ZOYA. Takes you back.

They heave RASHIDOV*'s body off.*

ANDROPOV. What I believe English aristocrats called 'the honourable course.'

GORBACHEV. Will we have to wait for all the gangsters to blow their brains out?

ANDROPOV *waves a hand, wearily.*

ANDROPOV. There were some things I could not tell the Politburo.

GORBACHEV. What? Why?

ANDROPOV. There was an attempt on my life last week.

A silence.

GORBACHEV. Serious?

ANDROPOV (*shrugs*). A machine gun nest. Near a road where they knew my car would pass. Discovered them just in time.

GORBACHEV. But who? Why?

ANDROPOV *looks away.*

ANDROPOV. I have lived the life of a primitive man, Mikhail Sergeyevich. Primitive times demanded it. (*He collects himself.*) The Moscow Mafia. The men who control the distribution of food in our capital city. They were informed of my movements. No doubt by their friends on the Politburo.

GORBACHEV. Grishin?

ANDROPOV *waves a hand.*

ANDROPOV. It's ironic. They need not have bothered.

They look at each other. ANDROPOV *smiles.*

I'm afraid so. The doctors say these kidneys will not see the end of the year.

Shock and grief upon GORBACHEV's *face.*

GORBACHEV. But surely . . .

ANDROPOV. No, let's not waste time. Listen carefully, Mikhail Sergeyevich. The laws of biology are on your side. This table will not give you a majority tomorrow, but the moment cannot be delayed indefinitely. The situation in the country is far too serious. Let Chernenko succeed, but exact a price. That price must be your succession. He'll be dead within the year.

GORBACHEV. You seem very sure?

ANDROPOV. As sure as the day when I demanded we put you on the Politburo.

GORBACHEV. I have always wondered about that. How were you so sure of me? I could have been running an underground racket in Stavropol. Just like the ones in Moscow.

For the only time in the scene, ANDROPOV *laughs.* GORBACHEV *looks at him slightly uneasily at first, but then he smiles.*

ANDROPOV. As head of the KGB, I knew the real situation in and out of the party, better than most. I had files on every leading party member. I knew the corrupt and the incorruptibles.

He pauses.

We did get a report on you once. A loan of several thousand roubles, was it? I can't recall.

GORBACHEV (*slightly pale*). Yes, yes , it was . . .

ANDROPOV. No need. You were clean! I checked. Sometimes, you know, my predecessors used to commission fake reports on Politburo members on whom they had nothing. Blackmail. I had all that rubbish pulped. (*He wags a finger.*) There are two thousand entries on the Politburo alone. You will need those files, Mikhail Sergeyevich.

GORBACHEV (*thinking aloud*). Tempo. That is the key. How fast?

ANDROPOV. What is important is not the pace of change, but what changes.

GORBACHEV. Speaking realistically, how much can we change?

ANDROPOV. Everything. There is no other choice.

GORBACHEV. Everything, Yuri Vladimirovich?

ANDROPOV. Listen to me, listen. For I have listened to *them*, for the last ten years. Listened, not to your experts in the Institutes, but to students of another university. The underground university. Literally. In the cellars of the Lubianka. We don't kill or torture them these days, we let them talk, let them write. For our own private library. Jewish dissidents, recalcitrant academicians, Ukrainian nationalists, religious maniacs funded by the CIA, smugglers who have become rouble millionaires and, my dear friend, members of the Lenin Clubs . . . you know, underground Left Communists. We even had a few deluded souls from Novocherkassk. Wanted to set up a free trade union.

GORBACHEV. Social malcontents? Riff-raff?

ANDROPOV. *No!* Understand. Vladimir Ilyich would have said that a lot of riff-raff were talking sense. That man was a supreme realist.

A pause.

You know, in a curious way, some of them reminded me of those Hungarian communists who were crushed by our tanks.

GORBACHEV. But the men around this table would never accept these arguments. You know that better than I do. Would they?

ANDROPOV. This table . . . (*A gesture.*) . . . has become the tombstone of all the hopes and dreams which were inspired by our young Soviet Republic. These men are hereditary gravediggers.

GORBACHEV. Are you really suggesting that the men around this table are dispensable?

ANDROPOV. Not just them. The table itself is dispensable.

GORBACHEV. And you have hidden all this inside yourself, for all these years?

ANDROPOV. The country *itself* has hidden all this inside itself for sixty years. And now the entire socialist cause, my entire life, is in danger of being suffocated to death by this . . . (*He indicates the table.*) . . . corpse.

GORBACHEV. What you're saying means a new revolution.

ANDROPOV. Yes.

GORBACHEV. But could we . . . should we . . . transplant the anarchy of your Lubianka cellars to . . . to society? This would . . .

ANDROPOV's fist falls upon the table.

ANDROPOV. That is why we need a revolution from above. If things get out of control, everything could go up in smoke. The ordinary people will be on our side against the bloated men of the apparatus. The problem you will confront is radical impatience amongst your own supporters. What did Vladimir Ilyich call it? (*A wistful smile upon his face.*) Left-wing communism: an infantile disorder. Leading this party is never easy. It will be especially difficult for you. Even painful. Because you will sometimes have to vote against your own best instincts and your close comrades in order to strengthen and safeguard the Soviet Union.

GORBACHEV. One more thing. (*He pauses.*) Why did Nikita Sergeyevich fail?

ANDROPOV sighs.

ANDROPOV. Why did Khrushchev fail? He showed audacity only once, when he denounced the crimes of Stalin in 1956. We needed it again and again and again. Khrushchev was destroyed because he was a man with a big heart but a small mind. He was all rhetoric and no tactics, the apparatus waited and then . . . . (*He makes a gesture.*) Your most dangerous moment will come when the people want you to break loose. Then you must decide quickly to trust them and break the back of the bureaucracy. If you miss the chance, you will not get another. Do you understand what I am saying?

They stare at each other. GORBACHEV nods in admiration. The lights go down. The lights go up. ZOYA, LENA and KATYA are throwing the wreaths back onto the table.

ZOYA. Maybe we lost a good one there.

LENA. Good one, bad one, good one, bad one, good one, bad . . .

KATYA. Lenin, Stalin, Khrushchev, Brezhnev, Andropov.

They look at each other, horror on their faces.

ZOYA. Grishin?

LENA. Ustinov?

KATYA. Chernenko?

And once again the members of the Politburo assemble around the table.

GRISHIN. I propose Comrade Chernenko for General Secretary.

The THREE WOMEN *look at each other.* KATYA *waves at the wreaths.*

KATYA. Let's leave them there.

The THREE WOMEN *go off.*

USTINOV. Good idea!

GROMYKO. Just a minute.

A silence.

We have just lost two General Secretaries.

A VOICE. But comrade Chernenko is in excellent health.

GROMYKO. I am aware that he is younger than Ronald Reagan. (*Looking at* USTINOV.) But none of us will see our youth again and our dear Konstantin Semyonovich whom comrade Grishin has proposed as General Secretary is like an over-ripe, rotting Georgian guava.

A shocked silence.

GRISHIN. Intolerable abuse, comrade Gromyko.

GROMYKO (*deadpan*). Political analysis. We must think of the country. We need a younger man. The party demands a younger man.

They all look at GORBACHEV.

GORBACHEV. I second the proposal to nominate comrade Chernenko.

GROMYKO. Agreed. But I insist on one thing. Comrade Gorbachev must be consulted before any major decision is taken. Agreed?

A VOICE. Dual power on the Politburo?

GROMYKO. Agreed.

They all nod, uneasily.

Then we vote.

A VOICE. But where is comrade Chernenko?

GRISHIN. On his way.

He waves off-stage. The THREE WOMEN *come on, fast, wheeling the coffin.* KATYA *wrinkles her nose at the smell.*

GROMYKO (*casually*). Let's vote.

They all look at GORBACHEV. *He raises his hand. They all raise their hands.* GRISHIN *goes to the coffin and raises* CHERNENKO's *hand.* USTINOV *peers into the coffin and shakes his head.*
Funeral music.
The members of the Politburo shuffle to the coffin, form a cortège and carry the coffin off.
GORBACHEV *remains alone in his seat.*

KATYA. Good one, bad one, good one, bad one, good one, bad one, good . . .

ZOYA. Lenin, Stalin, Khrushchev, Brezhnev, Andropov, Chernenko.

LENA. Gorbachev?

The THREE WOMEN *look at* GORBACHEV *and go off. He sits in silence. He stands. He walks to* LENIN's *chair and sits.*

GORBACHEV. We will now proceed to reconstruct the socialist order.

A pause.

And let us look forward to a time when there will be no more regiments of the condemned, carrying their burdens of pain into endless exile. New times, when the whistles of the trains will no longer sound like songs of separation.

He stands and steps up onto the table. A trap-door opens. He walks down beneath.

Scene Two

A trap-door opens. A very long queue climbs slowly up onto the table top.
KATYA, LENA *and* ZOYA *are in the queue.*
A long silence.

LENA. What's at the end of this queue?

KATYA. Someone said fish.

ZOYA. I was told meat.

A BYSTANDER. I thought it was coffee.

LENA. There hasn't been fish, meat or coffee in this shop for two
    years. I was told there was toilet paper.

ZOYA (*aside*). Patience is becoming a perishable commodity. Minds
    in the deep freeze for seventy years are beginning to thaw. This
    queue will soon get rough.

An American woman tourist, RONA ANDERSON, *comes on. She is
    fashionably dressed in 'Dr Zhivago' gear, with a full rig of Canon camera
    equipment about her neck. The queue stare at her, sullenly.*

RONA (*aside*). I really am, I really really am in Moscow in the age of
    glasnost! I'm staying at this *weird* hotel. It's got big Greek urns on
    the roof? With the hammer and sickle sticking out of them?
    Breakfast in that hotel was something else – there were Buddhist
    monks, and, ah, (*Low.*) Muslims, with veils? The Soviet Union's
    got Muslims with veils? (*Louder.*) And there were these wild guys.
    A Soviet heavy metal rock band. (*Low.*) The bass guitarist
    changed me ten roubles to the dollar. (*Loud.*) I mean I looked at
    my star chart, and I said, 'Rona, go to Moscow'. (*To the queue.*)
    Excuse me, is this the line for theatre tickets? (*The people in the
    queue stare at her.*)

A BYSTANDER. Strange how it used to be dangerous to talk to
    foreigners.

SECOND BYSTANDER. Now you just . . . don't want to talk to them.

RONA wanders off, taking pictures, saying . . .

RONA. Just look at that neat little church . . .

BORIS YELTSIN *comes on. He joins the queue at the back.*

KATYA. Oi! Look, him. Him.

LENA. What's he doing here?

ZOYA. Who?

LENA. Him. That's . . .

A BYSTANDER. What's a suit like that doing in a queue like this?

The queue moves fast and YELTSIN *is passed along the queue until he
    is at the front, confronting a* YOUNG WOMAN *in white.*

YELTSIN (*in stentorian tones*). Two kilos of veal, please Miss.

The YOUNG WOMAN *stares at him.* YELTSIN *turns so the whole queue can hear him.*

I said two kilos of veal, please Miss.

A BYSTANDER. Who's this joker? Why is he wasting our time?

SECOND BYSTANDER. Maybe he's escaped from the asylum.

YELTSIN *takes out his party card and shows it to the* YOUNG WOMAN.

YELTSIN. Get the manager! Now!

The MANAGER *comes forward.*

My name is Boris Nikolayevich Yeltsin. I am the First Secretary of the Moscow Party (*He half turns to the queue.*). At 7 a.m. this morning, two hundred kilos of fresh veal were delivered to your shop. Where is it?

The queue erupts.

LENA. The manager's messed his trousers. Look!

YELTSIN. Things are going to change!

YELTSIN *goes off to a round of applause. The supermarket* MANAGER *remains on stage. Three* GANGSTERS *walk onto the table.*

MANAGER. Flashed his party card at me! It was a trap.

FIRST GANGSTER. Shut up! You're not on the pay-roll to talk.

SECOND GANGSTER. What is this? The fucking Government, coming down to a queue?

THIRD GANGSTER. Wanted to know where the fucking veal was, did he? Didn't you tell him? In the kitchens of the Central Committee.

FIRST GANGSTER. What do we know about this Yeltsin?

SECOND GANGSTER. Was in the Urals, I think. Sverdlovsk. Brought in rationing there.

THIRD GANGSTER. I remember the bastard! Gave our boys a lot of trouble down there. Called us a Mafia. (*A twitch of pride.*) 'Soviet Mafia.'

FIRST GANGSTER. Can we put Yeltsin on the pay-roll?

The other two shake their heads.

SECOND GANGSTER. He really believes in all that crap.

FIRST GANGSTER. He what?

SECOND GANGSTER. That Soviet crap! Socialism? Remember that?

FIRST GANGSTER. Jesus. We can't have him running Moscow.

The THREE GANGSTERS *and the* MANAGER *go off.* YELTSIN *comes back on. He jumps up onto the table and addresses the queue.*

YELTSIN. Are you going to stand here all your lives? Do you know something? Two minutes away there's another shop. Everything's in there. Soap powder, Mum Champagne, fresh caviare from the Caspian Sea. And no queues. All I have to do is show this card . . . I can walk out with whatever I like.

A BYSTANDER (*mutters*). And what are you going to do about it, bigshot party boss?

YELTSIN. I heard that! I'll tell you what I'll do. What I want to do. Close down every special party shop in Moscow. Make the Politburo join the queue. Give them a taste of real life.

BYSTANDER. They'll just send their chauffeurs instead.

YELTSIN. Good point. Why the hell should we have chauffeurs? Special schools, special clinics, special this, special that, special holidays, special dachas in the countryside, special shopping in Paris. Oh yes! The party apparatus has achieved socialism. And sod the rest of you. Your future? Stay in the queue.

KATYA. Boris Nikolayevich. I would gladly join this queue every day, just to hear you talk. But we have to eat and drink.

ANOTHER. Promises have been made before.

AND ANOTHER. Kilos of promises. Piled up where the meat should be.

YELTSIN. I'll do my best. Of that you can be sure.

The queue queues on. GORBACHEV *and* YAKOVLEV *come on.*

GORBACHEV. Fourteen Second Secretaries. Fourteen, Boris Nikolayevich? Did you have to sack them all? The Moscow party is like a hornet's nest.

YELTSIN *laughs.*

YELTSIN. Dead flies! Dead flies! I'm the only hornet.

YAKOVLEV (*low*). Arrogance.

GORBACHEV *smiles*.

(*To* YELTSIN.) Can all fourteen be wrong, and only you right? By the law of averages, is that likely?

YELTSIN. More! It's certain. They were all corrupt. Time servers. Half of them are in the pocket of the Moscow Mafia. Grishin's creatures. Shit is shit. You, Mikhail Sergeyevich, you got rid of Grishin. And you expect me to work with what he left behind? They refused to accept my authority. Said I was the first leader of the Moscow party not a full member of the Politburo. And whose fault is that, comrades?

YAKOVLEV. Partially your own.

GORBACHEV. Boris you are turning up at every queue in Moscow. Exciting people. Making promises. Attacking the Politburo.

YELTSIN. Correction. Sections of the Politburo.

GORBACHEV. Boris Nikolayevich, I do not have a majority to make you a full member of the Politburo. Develop a sense . . . of timing. Tempo. Pace. Crucial in these situations.

YELTSIN. Today they gun for me, so tomorrow they can shoot you. Glasnost? Perestroika? They know what it means. If *we* win, they're finished. That's why they resist. Fourteen secretaries in Moscow is nothing. We've got to dump the lot.

YAKOVLEV. Sack? Dump? Get rid of? We are living in a period of glasnost. Differences in the party are normal. Purging the leadership is a habit of which we are trying to cure ourselves.

YELTSIN. Purge? Is a free election a purge? Elections, inside the party, at every level. That's the only purge I support. (*He glances at his watch.*) Now if you'll excuse me I'll have to go and answer questions at a Moscow party meeting.

GORBACHEV. Very little divides us, Boris. But try to co-operate with people more. To get them on your side.

YELTSIN. Are you beginning to patronize me?

He goes off.

YAKOVLEV. Perestroika's loose cannon.

GORBACHEV. But it is disturbing to hear someone voice your innermost thoughts.

YAKOVLEV. Even when the voice is from the bottom of a vodka bottle?

GORBACHEV *looks at him sharply.*

GORBACHEV. We all have our personal defects, Alexander Nikolayevich.

YAKOVLEV. But you know yours.

GORBACHEV. Meaning?

YAKOVLEV. Your faith that people can be reclaimed.

GORBACHEV *grunts.*

GORBACHEV. If you don't believe that, get out of Government service. (*Angrily.*) It is not a personal, or a political matter. Boris is one of us. He is a great believer. I like him. But he doesn't grasp the immensity of the problem. We have to make a vast desert bloom again, a desert the size of the Union of Soviet Socialist Republics.

YAKOVLEV (*softly*). For that to happen, we need a climatic change. Planet-wide.

GORBACHEV. Exactly.

YAKOVLEV. Can we deal with Reagan? The man's a criminal.

GORBACHEV. But he's lazy. And I am not.

They begin to walk off. RONA *wanders back on.*

YAKOVLEV. Talking of the reclamation of human beings, the economic commission has found out where all the sugar has gone.

GORBACHEV *grunts.*

YAKOVLEV. We raised the price of vodka in the anti-alcohol abuse campaign. So illegal vodka stills are everywhere.

GORBACHEV. Vodka needs a great deal of sugar . . .

YAKOVLEV. Ergo . . . (*A shrug.*) Why does the elegance of economics so often conspire with the ugly side of human nature? You encourage people not to be pissed out of their heads all the time. Result? No sugar in your tea.

GORBACHEV. The KGB can smash the illegal stills. It'll give them
    something to do. And we'll ration sugar, two kilos a month. (*They
    begin to walk off.*) And my dear comrade Yakovlev, stop theorising
    about human nature! There's too much to be done! The psyche of
    our country and its citizens has been traumatised. Ever since the
    thirties, we have not thought our own thoughts, we have
    deliberately blanked out our own minds. Once you betray yourself,
    you can betray anyone. Trust in oneself. That's what we have to
    build again. Without it, no glasnost. Unfortunately success does
    not depend on us alone. (*A pause.*) How do you think the West will
    respond?

Before YAKOVLEV *can reply, they are interrupted by* RONA.

RONA. Mr Gorbachev? Excuse me, Mr President Sir. I can answer
    your last question. I wouldn't worry yourself. Nancy and Ron
    Reagan will soon drop this Evil Empire nonsense. From next
    month on you'll only find the Evil Empire in the movies. You know
    the movies always take a few years to catch up with the real world.
    (*She pats him on the back.*) You just stay with it.

YAKOVLEV (*ultra politely*). Thank you, madam. It's very gratifying
    that ordinary American people are beginning to see what we're
    trying to do. Thank you.

RONA. Hey, I'm no ordinary tourist. I'm Nancy Reagan's astrologer.
    And the news I'm getting from up here . . . (*She points to the sky.*) is
    that we can do business with you. I'm serious. Do you wanna know
    what I'm going to tell my President when I get back?

GORBACHEV *and* YAKOVLEV *nod.* RONA *lets her raincoat drop to
    the floor revealing Jane Fonda leotards. She then begins to sing and dance
    a Jane Fonda work out routine.*

Rona's Peace Song

RONA. Mr President!
    Get one thing in your head
    Get one thing in your head
    Kremlinology is dead
    Kremlinology is dead
    You don't need it any more
    To tell you there's a mess
    We can read it every day
    In the Soviet press.
    Stars in the sky
    So bright and clear

Every night they whisper
In my ear
Mr President
Peace is near
Peace is near.

*She bows. GORBACHEV and YAKOVLEV applaud and laugh. She
shakes hands with both men and strides off. GORBACHEV and
YAKOVLEV look up at the sky, then at each other. They go off.
The queue shuffles forward.*
*GRISHA, an old man in his seventies but still full of health, walks across
the table briskly. He stares at the queue. Then ZOYA sees him. A look of
horror passes over her face.*

GRISHA. Zoya come home.

ZOYA. No.

GRISHA. Come home now.

*A pause. Then she leaves the queue. He takes her by the arm and they walk,
her body awkward and stiff.*
*They go off, passing the THREE GANGSTERS on the way. They are
accompanied by RIMMA, a woman in Politburo uniform.*

FIRST GANGSTER. First it was the meat, then it was the milk. Yeltsin
is totally out of control. He's disrupting everything! How long 'til
you move against him, how long Rimma Zhukova?

RIMMA. We're working on it. He's upsetting people at the very top.
But you must be patient.

SECOND GANGSTER. Patient? This is a huge operation, supplying
the secretaries of thirty-three fucking committees.

THIRD GANGSTER. And that's just in Moscow.

SECOND GANGSTER. You top party members won't be patient,
when there's no more steak . .

FIRST GANGSTER. Caviare . . .

THIRD GANGSTER. The odd Sony Walkman thrown in, the odd
foreign video . .

FIRST GANGSTER. Not to mention, meat, fruit 'n' veg . . .

SECOND GANGSTER. Real coffee . . .

THIRD GANGSTER. Soap . . .

SECOND GANGSTER. Toothpaste . . .

FIRST GANGSTER. All delivered, straight to your home, no
  questions asked. What's the matter with you party officials? Don't
  you want the benefits of socialism any more?

RIMMA. I've told you, we're working on it. Leave it to us.

FIRST GANGSTER. How long?

RIMMA. It will happen soon. And now understand one thing. Never
  contact me like this again. Yeltsin's friends have eyes.

She goes off, quickly. The GANGSTERS *laugh.*

THIRD GANGSTER. She's ashamed of us.

The THREE GANGSTERS *go off. The queue shuffles forward. Whispers
begin.*

VOICES IN THE QUEUE. What? What? What is it? . . . Tea, tea, tea . .
  . What? . . . There's tea, round the corner . . . Always they do this.
  They get something in the shop, they sell it round the corner in
  the street! . . . Tea! Round the corner! Tea!

*The queue shuffles then begins to move. A trap opens, the queue hurries
down it beneath the stage.*

Scene Three

*A trap opens. A small round table, covered by a red cloth and lace. Upon the
table, a vase of dried flowers and a vodka bottle, untouched.*
GRISHA, ZOYA *and* BORIS, *their thirty-year-old son. All three of them
have been crying.* ZOYA *is clutching an envelope to her bosom.*
A silence, ZOYA *moving from one foot to the other, with a swaying motion.*

BORIS. Mother, open it.

GRISHA. Zoya, open it. (*He holds out his hand for the letter.*)

BORIS. He was my brother.

GRISHA. My son! At least General Gromov sent us the letter,
  personally. At least there is some comfort in knowing there is one
  Red Army General who cares for his soldiers.

  ZOYA *flings the envelope at them.*

ZOYA. Comfort? Comfort? And *your* son? You bastard! I hate you.
  Don't you ever call him your son. I pleaded with you, I went down

on my knees. Don't let them send him. No one else in your position let their sons go. But not you, oh no. Fifty years a secret policeman. You couldn't abuse your position. And now he's dead. My little Andrushka is dead. (*To* BORIS, *with a gesture at* GRISHA.) He wouldn't lift a finger to save his son. He's the only one in there, in Dzerzhinsky Square, who believes in all this . . . I had to carry on working as a cleaner. You would go to the local school. My Andrei would go to Afghanistan. Your pure, your incorruptible father! Do you know who this man is? He's a torturer. A murderer. Ask him what he's been doing for fifty years. GPU, NKVD, KGB. Doing their dirty work.

BORIS (*stunned*). Father, what's she talking about? You work as a janitor, in the Mayakovsky Museum. You always have. In . . . (*He hesitates.*) Dzerzhinsky Square.

ZOYA. That's what he wanted you children to think. Actually he worked across the street, in the Lubianka.

BORIS. But we'd go and see you, in the Museum. Tell me it's not true. I remember the day Gorbachev was elected General Secretary, you proposed a toast. You looked really happy. I don't understand. Grief has deranged her. Don't listen to her. Father?

GRISHA. In those days . . . you had to be alone. Deaf. Separated from your family. Detached from yourself.

ZOYA. Don't be coy. Tell him what your job was, you bastard!

A pause.

GRISHA. The day I joined. I was, what, sixteen or seventeen? The very first day, they made me sit in a room. Meyerhold was being tortured. I had been to his theatre, I'd seen all his plays. Been inspired, moved, laughed and wept. I remember the day when Trotsky, fresh from the front, interrupted a play about the Civil War and clambered onto the stage, to give us the latest news. The actors were petrified. We cheered. And now they were breaking Meyerhold's fingers, one by one. Urine was being poured on his head. 'You Jews stick together don't you' they shouted. He had dedicated one of his plays to Trotsky. I saw him die. They hammered a bolt into his head. I was sick. I felt ill. I still dream about him.

ZOYA. Tell him what your job was!

GRISHA. Alright! I'll hide nothing.

A pause.

They saw me reading novels. So I was put in charge of the arrested writers and artists. I was blunt with them. They were going to die anyway. What was the point of torture? They might as well confess and save themselves the trouble. I told them what happened to the veins in the temples of the electrocuted. Oh yes, I was very convincing.

BORIS. But why?

GRISHA. I was a Bolshevik. A disciplined communist. It was dirty work, but it had to be done. The Revolution had to be saved. They were bad times, young Boris. There was cannibalism in the Ukraine during the collectivisation. Children were being eaten. Whenever my mother went out to forage for food, your Aunt Halina, who was then five years old, was handcuffed to the leg of the table. Just in case a neighbour decided to steal her for supper.

BORIS. Better to die of hunger than torture innocents to death.

GRISHA. Easy, easy to say! But morality never entered into it. We had lost a few million during the First World War. Then came the civil war. Millions more died. People were tired. They wanted stability. A rest.

BORIS. The only peace you gave them was the peace of the graveyard.

GRISHA (*ignoring him*). One day they brought me a poet. Fellow by the name of Osip Mandelstam. He had recited a poem about Stalin at an informal gathering. In his own house. We were informed. Stalin was a sado-masochist. He took a perverse pleasure in reading attacks upon himself. Stalin wanted the poem. I explained our problem to Mandelstam. He had recited the poem by heart, the only copy was in his head. At first he denied the poem's existence. Then I told him who had informed. That shook him. He asked for some paper. I gave him enough for two copies, one for Stalin, one for our files. I sat there with him as he wrote, wanting to say something intimate. Something simple. A word of encouragement. I knew his poetry well. He wrote out his Stalin poem, the two copies, handed them to me. 'Here,' he said. 'Let the bastard read it. It'll make my death worthwhile.' I felt like hugging him. Those words. The subterranean emotions. They have remained, imprinted on my brain ever since.

He recites.

Our lives no longer feel ground underneath them
Ten steps away you can't hear our words.

But whenever there's a snatch of talk
It turns to the Kremlin mountaineer,
The ten thick worms of his fingers,
His words like measures of weight,
The huge laughing cockroaches on his top lip,
The glitter of his boot-rims.

Ringed with the scum of chicken-necked bosses
He toys with the tributes of half-men.
One whistles, another miaows, a third snivels.
He pokes out his finger and he alone goes boom.
He forges decrees in a line like horseshoes
One for the groin, one the forehead, temple, eye,
He rolls the executions on his tongue like berries.
He wishes he could hug them like big friends from home.

A silence.

BORIS. Mother, the letter.

A pause.

The letter, mother.

ZOYA (*opens the letter and reads*). 'My dearest Mama. By the time you
   get this I'll be on my way home and this hot, parched city with its
   mudbrick houses and its gardens and its oriental coffee houses,
   and its silver sickle rising over the small minarets will just be a
   memory. There's a strong rumour that Gorbachev will bring us all
   home. We all want that. It's another world here. There's no
   Moscow behind us. There's no enemy trampling our fields.
   Yesterday I saw what they left of Misha. You remember Misha, the
   freckle-faced fatty who was my friend at school. You always
   grumbled that when he came round he ate up all the home-made
   jam. I met up with him here after all those years. We talked about
   being boys in Lefortovo, he made me laugh so much. Three weeks
   ago he was captured by the Dushman, the word here for the
   enemy. I wish he'd died before they got him. They flayed his skin
   off while he was alive. Then they chopped off his genitals and
   stuffed them down his throat. That's how we found him. Some of
   the lads were vomiting. I just wept and wept.
      For a few days what they did to Misha made me want to stay. If
   those bastards come to power that's what they'll do to anyone who
   disagrees with them. I have an Afghan friend , a soldier named
   Khalid. I see sadness in his eyes now that he knows we will all
   return soon. He's sad, though he says he's happy for me.
      The news from home is wonderful. We get the papers, it must be

so exciting. I have one last patrol on top of a red, hot hill. My love
to you all. I can't wait. Your Andrei. (*She folds the letter.*) My son is
dead, age twenty-three. Condemned by his youth and by those old
bastards round that table which I clean every day. Old vultures
who have lived too long.

BORIS. My brother is dead, without ever having known love or the
joys of life. Condemned to die in a war that was doomed from the
very start. And the men who sent him there will never be tried.

ZOYA *and* BORIS *look at* GRISHA.

GRISHA. My Andrei is dead in the springtime of his youth and my
heart is full of fury and suffering. I am an old man with not many
years to go.

*He goes to the small table and grasps it with both hands, leaning forward,
head bowed. Then he pours himself a glass of vodka. He raises it in a silent
toast and drains the glass. He speaks with a hard edge in his voice.*

(*Aside.*) Drive your plough and horses over the bones of the dead. I
have always believed that. It is hard and the dead are many. But
those who grieve for them will, in turn pass away . . . and all things
will be well. What else could I do, but to believe that? There is
much to be done.

BORIS. Tell me, you old man, you sad old man. Is Marxism
scientific?

GRISHA. No. If it were they'd have tried it on animals first.

A pause.

BORIS. OK. You've heard the latest quip going around Moscow.

GRISHA (*with fury*). Of course I have heard the latest Moscow quip! I
hear everything. I am a secret policeman!

BORIS. Yes. And even when you die, will your corpse spy on us from
the grave?

GRISHA. I . . .

GRISHA *cannot speak, exhausted. He descends upon a trap, still at the
table as, by another trap,* LENA *and* KATYA *climb up upon the stage from
another trap. They carry mops, brooms and pails.*

LENA. What's happened?

KATYA. Is it Andrei?

ZOYA *nods. The other two dump their things and embrace her, helping her from the stage.*

Scene Four

Reykjavik. GORBACHEV, *in winter clothing, is looking out to sea.* SECURITY MEN *keep watch.* LENIN *appears in mid-air.*

GORBACHEV. Look at this landscape. Bleak, like another planet.

LENIN. Volcanic Iceland. Young, still being made by force of nature. But the human will is part of nature, and as strong.

GORBACHEV. You had every confidence that it is. What do you make of Ronald Reagan?

LENIN. Bah! (*An irritable wave of his arm.*) You must give up these imaginary conversations with me, Mikhail Sergeyevich. I am, after all, dead.

GORBACHEV. We have been having imaginary conversations with you for nearly seventy years, Vladimir Ilyich. You seem to have more to say dead, than you did when you were alive.

LENIN. That's because you've not buried me properly. Just *when* are you going to end that obscenity beside the Kremlin wall?

GORBACHEV. Soon.

LENIN. Will the Russians ever cure themselves of religious mania? I let them have the monastery at Zagorsk, to kiss their icons. Then my own comrades embalmed me like a saint. Reagan is in a state of shock. (*He laughs, slaps his leg.*) Have a little human feeling! You've punched the old man in the face. Wham! You propose cutting the number of strategic weapons, by half. *Then* you accept their own zero option – all intermediate warheads out of Europe. No frills, no tricks! Reagan only put the zero option in 1981, because he thought the USSR would never agree. They are not used to Soviets saying 'yes'. *Then* you tell him you want an agreement on no nuclear weapons in space, under the ABM treaty. Have a heart, Mikhail Sergeyevich. You're doing something terrible to the Americans. You are depriving them of an enemy. What will they do without the barbarian at the gate?

GORBACHEV. Mmm.

He pauses.

This morning, when we put our three proposals to him, there was a terrible sensation. You sensed it, hovering in the air above the table . . . (*An exasperated gesture.*) We have prepared for this summit. When meeting with an American President we have learnt to expect a criminal mind. Kennedy was a mafioso chieftan of the American monied class, Johnson, well . . . And Richard Nixon had a criminal mind of an almost profound depth . . .

LENIN (*dreamily*). Yes, even poor Jimmy Carter behaved like a peasant farmer on the fiddle. I always found there was a certain advantage in dealing with crooks . . .

GORBACHEV. But with Reagan . . . His innocence is almost plausible. Plausible in its banality. He complained to George Shultz that my briefcase had more papers than his did. For an hour, that's all he could think of, while we proposed the dismantling of vast nuclear arsenals! He doesn't understand, he really does just want to talk about old American movies.

LENIN. The Romans made a horse their Emperor – a horse, a cowboy from Hollywood as a head of state . . . why not? Don't underestimate Reagan. He has defeated every American politician who ever opposed him. He stays within the boundaries of what he knows, that is why he is so effective. If you can deal direct with the old fart you may get somewhere. Your problem is his advisers.

GORBACHEV. You're right. We must not get distracted. Even if Ronald Reagan does ride into the afternoon session in a saddle. (*He looks at his watch.*) Lunchtime is nearly over. The Americans will be out of the portable bubble they call their 'secure facility' . . .

LENIN. Which you are bugging with radio waves at a frequency they did not conceive of . . .

GORBACHEV. We will ask for a response to our three proposals, one by one. Concise, clear. (*He clenches his gloved fists by his sides.*) Reagan operates within what he knows. But we are in unknown territory.

He turns to go.

LENIN. One thing.

GORBACHEV *stops*.

You always say 'we', never 'I'. This is not the Royal 'we', I know, it's the *collective* 'we'. But it is fucking irritating.

GORBACHEV. Saying 'we' has become a Soviet habit.

LENIN. When I had something to say, I always said 'I'.

GORBACHEV. I . . . (*He bristles, fists clenched.*) I want my conscience to be clear.

LENIN. You can be something of a stuffed shirt, Mikhail Sergeyevich. Watch that.

GORBACHEV. I do. (*He relaxes. He rams the fist of his right hand into the palm of his left. He smiles.*) We do.

He walks away. Lights down, and up. Night-time. The SECURITY MEN *are still there. Strong searchlights from the wings sweep the grass, that is the table top, then are still.*

LENIN. You will get rid of me, you know, if you succeed. There will be something called 'De-Leninisation'.

GORBACHEV. Not yet.

LENIN. Not yet not yet, soon soon, not yet. I never set out to 'Leninise'. I just sought to lead the working class. (*He laughs, swinging his legs.*) Meanwhile abroad there are American bombs and at home the shoes in the shops are shit. So how are you getting on, Mikhail Sergeyevich?

GORBACHEV. Deadlock. (*An irritable gesture.*) These negotiations are like a brawl in a kindergarten. We know they know half their old missiles would never get out of their silos . . .

LENIN. And they must know half *our* missiles are made of wood. For the benefit of their spy satellites.

An affronted glance from GORBACHEV.

GORBACHEV. Not as many as half, Vladimir Ilyich.

LENIN. Mmm. How do you know, sat behind a Kremlin desk? (*He sags, legs splayed.*) Give them everything they want.

GORBACHEV. I can't . . .

LENIN. Give the West everything they want. Give yourself the chance to rebuild socialism in the Soviet Union.

A pause.

GORBACHEV. I can't.

LENIN (*angrily*). That was my policy! The Treaty of Brest-Litovsk. I got the young Soviet Republic out of the First World War, gave the

Kaiser's German Empire everything it wanted. Where is the
Kaiser's Empire now? Dust.

GORBACHEV. We cannot allow the Americans to develop star wars.

LENIN. Bah! Starwars, a comic book fantasy. It will never work. Let
Reagan play Luke Skywalker, while we get on with building the real
world.

GORBACHEV. I cannot.

LENIN. Ah Misha Misha, this is your great flaw. You assume that
other people are as intelligent as you. Let the Yanks twiddle with
their star wars. And you'll win everything.

GORBACHEV. I cannot.

LENIN. The whole summit will collapse.

A silence.

GORBACHEV. My conscience is clear.

A silence. Then LENIN, *chirpily.*

LENIN. Fine, fine. You'll get an INF agreement next year, when
Reagan's got over the shock of this weekend. The cruise missiles in
Europe will be withdrawn. (*A shrug.*) They too would never work,
but it's something. But . . . (*Suddenly hard in his voice.*) Time,
Mikhail Sergeyevich. Don't run out of time.

LENIN *slides away through the air.*

Scene Five

KATYA, LENA *and* ZOYA, *cleaning the table.*
The POLITBURO *enters with new faces.* GRISHIN, ROMANOV *and*
USTINOV *have gone. In their place* LIGACHEV *and* YAKOVLEV,
SHEVARDNADZE, RYZHKOV *and* ZAIKOV.
ZAIKOV *is a classic man of the apparatus, a 'grey spot'.*
GORBACHEV *is walking to* LENIN*'s chair when* KATYA *waylays him.*

KATYA. Comrade Gorbachev! When will our boys return from
Afghanistan?

GORBACHEV. Soon, soon. Why? Do you have a son there?

KATYA. No. She (*Points to* ZOYA.) had a son there. He won't be coming back.

> GORBACHEV *walks to* ZOYA *and holds her hand in his. He leans forward and speaks a few words to her, unheard. Members of the Politburo look uneasy.*

LENA (*to* KATYA, *sotto*). Oh he does that. He walks into crowds and has a few words. He's good at doing that.

KATYA. Yes. The five year plan is going well.

LENA. What plan?

KATYA. The five year plan for fine words.

LENA (*to* ZOYA). What did he say?

ZOYA. Patience.

KATYA. There you are! That's a fine word.

> *The* THREE WOMEN *go off.* GORBACHEV *sits in* LENIN'*s chair.*

GORBACHEV. Is he here?

> LIGACHEV *nods.*

Ask him to come in.

> *An exhausted, rather shambolic* YELTSIN *comes on. He looks only at* GORBACHEV, *who motions him to an empty chair.* YELTSIN *sits. A pause.*

GORBACHEV. Comrade Yeltsin, thank you for coming to this meeting. I'm aware you've not been well. This need not take long. There is a motion before the Politburo concerning your case.

YELTSIN. Case? Am I now a case?

GORBACHEV. The meeting of the Moscow Executive voted to remove you as First Secretary. They've asked us to approve their decision and to simultaneously remove you as a candidate member of the Politburo. Is there anything you wish to say?

> YELTSIN *rises to his feet, but he is exhausted and falls back again.* SHEVARDNADZE *hands him a glass of water. He gulps it down. A pause.*
> *Then he rises to his feet again.*

YELTSIN. The Moscow Executive! A joke. The whole thing was organised by you, Comrade Ligachev, aided and abetted by the Central Committee apparatus. I don't have to tell you about the

Moscow Committee. From the day I took over there has been
sabotage. We had millions of kilos of farm and garden produce
brought in, to fill the city's supermarkets. It was left to rot.
Trainloads of food from the Caucasus were sent back, unloaded.
What is the smell of the state of the union? The stench of uneaten
food rising from goods yards. And mingling with it, a human stink.
The Moscow Committees are sumps of corruption. The sewers of
conservatism, full of rats and gangsters . . . Bribes. Intimidation.
They can see the world in no other way. A First Secretary of the
Zhdanov District came to see me, you know her, Rimma Zhukova.
'Poison Rimma', as she is known to ordinary people. She was
upset. Know why? Because I wanted to end the Mafia control over
milk and meat in Moscow. She said 'If you want to finish the Mafia
off you'll have to settle with me too'. A party member, a so-called
servant of the people, threatening me on behalf of gangsters.
Blatant. Shameless. We have invented something more deadly
than a medieval court, more deadly than the Borgias – the
apparatus of the Soviet nomenklatura.

LIGACHEV. This is demagogy . . .

GORBACHEV. Comrade Ligachev, let him finish.

LIGACHEV (*with a wan smile*). Yes, let him talk.

YELTSIN *is exhausted, leaning forward with his fists on the table.
He pauses.*

YELTSIN. I have to speak of these things, though they be like
kerosene in the mouth.

ZAIKOV (*sotto*). And that's not all his breath smells of.

LIGACHEV *sniggers.* YELTSIN *looks up, again flooded with energy.*

YELTSIN (*at* LIGACHEV). No one can accuse *me* of being a rat in the
corner, of muttering my true opinions in secret.

LIGACHEV *stiffens.*

YELTSIN. Comrades, we want the people to make more sacrifices, as
if they hadn't made enough already, but fair enough. To revitalise
the economy a shakeout is necessary. We have to win over the
workers, the housewives, ordinary citizens. The powerless in our
society must come to power, whatever the pain that may cause to
us who ride in limousines! I do not believe that people will agree to
any sacrifice as long as the nomenklatura exists. We must abolish
special privileges for the apparatus, yes for us! Then we might be
taken more seriously. Comrade Ligachev here sees himself as the

guardian of the apparatus, his mouth moves and says 'perestroika', but his hands throttle the reforms. He is the strangler, doing the gangsters' work.

ZAIKOV. Disgraceful slanders!

YELTSIN. Crisis management of the apparatus will not work. It is an economic, a human disaster. Politically, a disaster as great as Chernobyl. Sweep the lot aside! All the top soil has to be dug up and dumped, as we've had to do in the Ukraine and Byelorussia. Comrade Ligachev, you do not behave as the number two leader should. The apparatus is the only world you know, you manoeuvre, you manipulate, protect a corrupt rascal here, promote a gutless time-server there. You speed with your kind in Zil limousines along the streets of this city, ignorant of the people, with the little curtains on the car's windows closed. I got a letter from one of your friends the other day. Here! (*He waves a letter.*)

ZAIKOV. Outrageous!

YELTSIN. Don't worry, I'm not saying it's from you. It's too poetic. (*He reads.*) 'Boris Nikolayevich, do not castigate us. Do you not see it is futile? We are the élite and you will not break society's stratification. You do not have enough strength. We will rip apart the feeble wings of your perestroika. You will not reach your destination, so restrain your ardour.' There speaks the apparatus. Confident. Contemptuous. Ruthless.

He is exhausted. He slumps into his chair. LIGACHEV *leans back. He speaks calmly.*

LIGACHEV. Boris, Boris, St George fighting the dragon of corruption. (*He smiles.*) But you have been stabbing the Politburo in the back for several months. Haranguing shop queues? Calling meetings of the Moscow party? Closing down special shops without consulting any leading body?

YELTSIN (*muttering angrily*). Leading body, leading body, bodies leading bodies, leading body . . .

LIGACHEV. If perestroika is to succeed we must be united. Your treacherous behaviour fuels the activities of the unscrupulous. Your grand gestures are, objectively, reactionary. It's you who encourage the enemies of our party. Enemies of the Revolution. Political adventurism and Bonapartism are not unknown in our party. We have dealt with such types before.

YELTSIN. Ah, the dead language! The phrases from Stalin's time, 'objective reaction', 'adventurism', 'Bonapartism', they're like boils on your lips, comrade. 'Types', ah yes, I'm one of them! Stalin knew how to deal with 'types' like me, eh? (*He pulls his finger across his throat. He is feeling increasingly more ill. He stops to drink more water.*)

(*To* GORBACHEV.) They've got my head, Mikhail Sergeyevich, but please be careful. They're flattering you mercilessly and you're only human. You go round the world. People in other countries compare you to their leaders and sigh with envy. Not that there's much competition about these days, there's no Churchill, Roosevelt or de Gaulle around. So our Mikhail is flattered. Now, I ask myself where is all this leading? I'll tell you, comrade, to your face. My fear is that the apparatus will integrate you and, for that matter, your wife.

SHEVARDNADZE. Boris!

YELTSIN. I will speak my mind. The style of Raisa Maximovna is alien to our movement. Wives have not played that type of part in our political world. Krupskaya did not use her position as Lenin's companion to demand special treatment. Stalin's wife, the much lamented Nadezhda Aliluyeva, made her voice heard by committing suicide. Nina Khrushchev, again a great woman, never behaved like the First Lady. Comrade Andropov's wife was seen once. At his funeral. In tears. But Raisa . . . rings me up at my office all the time, to make this or that request. Why? All this nonsense must stop. Are we to have a red Nancy Reagan? I am with you all the way, Mikhail Sergeyevich. But it will be a sad day if they build a personality cult around you. Criticism of Gorbachev is a forbidden zone. Beware the forked tongues of sycophants. Beware the twisted logic of the apparatus.

He slumps and falls as if he has had a heart attack. Everyone sits still. Then GORBACHEV *rushes to him first. Then* SHEVARDNADZE *and* YAKOVLEV. *They lift him and give him water. He recovers and takes his seat.*

GORBACHEV. We have discussed this matter long enough. The motion is clear. The Politburo confirms the decision of the Moscow Executive concerning comrade Yeltsin. In keeping with that decision, the Politburo feels that comrade Yeltsin's continued candidature of this body is now inappropriate. All those in favour.

Every hand goes up. YELTSIN *prepares to leave, furious.*

Comrade Yeltsin, we all know where we have to go, but sometimes you forget where we are starting from.

YELTSIN, *walking slowly from his chair.*

YELTSIN. Careful, Mikhail Sergeyevich. With this gang around you there's no telling where you might end up.

LIGACHEV. I propose we recommend the candidature of comrade Zaikov as First Secretary to the Moscow Executive.

YELTSIN *turns and shouts.*

YELTSIN. There's your reply Mikhail Sergeyevich. This is how they operate. Zaikov, one of their creatures. Let Zaikov contest an election against me in Moscow. Let the people decide. Of course you won't! (*He laughs.*) He'll be destroyed. And it would set an unhealthy precedent. (*To* GORBACHEV, *privately.*) Why so cold to me?

GORBACHEV (*angrily*). Because you're out of control, undisciplined, and you just don't understand. (*He goes off.*)

As YELTSIN *walks off he meets the* THREE WOMEN.

KATYA. Don't give up, Boris Nikolayevich. Moscow is behind you. Fight the bastards.

ZOYA. We don't mind if you fall down drunk in the rain, now and then. We don't mind that you've got a little Tartar mistress a third of your age.

LENA. Boris Nikolayevich, you must do what you think is right, but trust us. We don't want to lose again.

YELTSIN. No. The Soviet people can't afford another defeat. I promise you, I won't let you down. I'll do all I can, I'll give my life, I . . . (*He stops. He is weeping. Then he rushes from the stage.*)

KATYA. He was crying.

LENA. I don't think . . . that's a very good sign.

ZOYA. No. Let him cry. Not enough tears. During the bad years we used to laugh a lot, remember? Oh how we laughed to show the world that we were really happy. Even at home we had to laugh for fear of the informers in our midst. Our own children! So let him cry. It's a sign that times have changed.

They go off.

Scene Six

*A large bed comes up on a trap in the table. By the bed, a table: a lamp, a
telephone and a pile of books upon it. There are two clothes-stands: hanging on
one the* GORBACHEV *suit, coat, scarf and hat; on the other a very* RAISA
GORBACHEV *fur-trimmed coat. Sitting up in the bed, with large pillow
bolsters behind them and in their nightclothes, are* GORBACHEV *and his
wife,* RAISA. *He, reading-glasses on, is scribbling on official papers. She is
reading a book.*

RAISA. So good. So good.

   GORBACHEV *flicks a paper irritably.*

   You should certainly use this in your speech. The English poet
   Shelley. Listening?

   He takes off his glasses and nods, still holding a sheaf of papers. RAISA
   recites with flair.

   An old, mad, despised and dying king,
   Princes, the dregs of their dull race, who flow
   Through public scorn – mud from a muddy spring –
   Rulers who neither see, nor feel, nor know,
   But leech-like to their fainting country cling,
   Till they drop, blind in blood, without a blow –
   A people starved and stabbed in the untilled field –

GORBACHEV (*interrupting*). For my speech to the Americans in
   Malta? We're trying to be nice to them.

RAISA. No. Your speech to the Supreme Soviet.

   He smiles, wags a finger.

GORBACHEV. Ah. (*He puts his glasses back on. He almost rips a paper,
   angrily.*) We have the greatest intelligence service in the world.
   Endless intelligence of the latest stupidity.

   A pause.

RAISA. What a strange American film that was we watched tonight.

GORBACHEV (*writing*). 'Ghostbusters.'

RAISA. A goddess representing the third-world is gang-raped by
   maniacs with illegal nuclear weapons. Just entertainment.

GORBACHEV. It reflects their national preoccupations. If we
   succeed that could change . . . a little.

RAISA. Robert Redford as Mike Gorbachev!

GORBACHEV. Sigourney Weaver as Raisa the Siberian temptress!

RAISA. Boris Karloff as Boris Yeltsin.

They look at each other and laugh. GORBACHEV's foul mood returns.

GORBACHEV. This KGB report. Siberian coal miners have formed a
strike committee, because they have no soap. No soap! What will I
be reduced to? Standing up in the Supreme Soviet, thumping my
fist and shouting 'Let there be soap', to a standing ovation? I know
with what result – not one extra bar, not one . . . single . . . soap
bubble. What kind of fool will that make me look?

He stares at his hands, flexing his fingers.

Sakharov says there's too much power in my hands. If only that
were true. I'd make the bloody soap myself!

RAISA. Misha, for you perestroika means 'more soap', but for many
it means 'more God'. Russians have always neglected cleanliness
for godliness. I loathe religion. If we could sell off our godliness for
hard currency, this country would be rich.

GORBACHEV. Soap. God. Power. (*He lifts another paper and lets it slide
from his fingers.*) Another report. Azerbaijani nationalists are
blockading all trains carrying relief supplies into Armenia for the
earthquake victims. Food, clothing, medicine, building materials,
everything. Is that to do with God, too? (*His shoulders droop.*) What
are people feeling out there? Tonight, what are they feeling, what
are they thinking?

RAISA *closes her book. A pause.*

RAISA. Have you seen the Top Secret File from the KGB in London?

GORBACHEV (*alarmed*). What file?

RAISA. It's all over the Kremlin dining room. The file on why that
woman expelled our diplomats from our London Embassy.

GORBACHEV. What!

RAISA. That's it there.

GORBACHEV *pulls out a folder.*

It's very interesting. The only way she can make love to Mr Denis is
by painting a little strawberry mark on his head. Just there.

GORBACHEV. Raisa Maximovna!

Simultaneously a blackout and a loud explosion. Lights up on an area at the edge of the table. Night. GRISHA, LARISSA *and* BORIS. *Their faces, hands and clothes are blackened.*

GRISHA. Out! Now! Get out!

BORIS. What happened to us? We were sitting at a table . . .

GRISHA. Out!

LARISSA (*off the table*). No, I'm alright.

BORIS. Sitting at a table, eating . . .

GRISHA. They fire-bombed the place.

BORIS *accepts* GRISHA'*s hand and gets off the table.*

LARISSA. We must help back there . . .

GRISHA. No! Leave it to the militia. There may be another device.

LARISSA (*very upset*). Who would do such a thing? While people are eating and drinking? It's an outrage! This is Moscow, not Beirut . . .

GRISHA. Maybe now they'll pay their protection money on time.

LARISSA *stares at him.* GRISHA *shrugs.*

Eat in a co-operative restaurant and you get something extra in the pancakes. (*Suddenly angry.*) It's a co-op! A private business! What do you expect? Free enterprise has its underbelly . . . with Al Capones hanging at its teats.

LARISSA. Don't you want the co-ops to work?

GRISHA. Of course. I'm a Gorbachev man.

BORIS. A KGB Gorbachev man.

LARISSA (*to herself*). The men are going to talk politics, the men are going to talk politics, the woman is expected to fall silent. God, this is a primitive country. (*To the men.*) Let's go home.

GRISHA. No. We must wait for the militia, we're witnesses. And good citizens, no?

LARISSA. Standing at night in a Moscow street, ash on my clothes, in my hair. What is happening to my country? For years we were told 'what we have is the best in the world' . . . best train engines, best spaceships, best teapots, the best . . . and now, Glasnost, and we know we've got the worst, worst shops, worst farms, worst power stations, worst train engines, worst stereo equipment and even one in three electric samovars don't work . . .

A WAITER, *similarly blackened, comes out with a tray, upon it three tumblers of wine.*

WAITER. Sorry about that in there. Please, with the compliments of the management.

GRISHA. What's going on?

LARISSA *and* BORIS *take a glass.* GRISHA *shakes his head.*

BORIS. Great. By the way the chicken was excellent, until it got bombed.

WAITER. Thank you man. We hope this won't put you off the restaurant.

BORIS. Not at all.

LARISSA. No . . .

WAITER. We'll be open again within the week. (*The* WAITER, *going off jauntily.*) See you around, folks.

GRISHA. Extraordinary behaviour!

BORIS. It's called 'good service'. It goes with capitalism. It doesn't mean anything. (*He sips.*) Georgian wine, and the best.

GRISHA. Strange days. But we must have patience.

BORIS *splutters at his wine.*

BORIS. Patience? Patience?

GRISHA. Yes patience.

BORIS. Oh yes, take the Gorbachev line, as you took every other line over the years. How many lines, how many years, Father?

LARISSA (*to herself*). Lines lines . . . lies lies . . . (*To* GRISHA.) He's right. Always my parents were asked to live with grand schemes! But what about living the little scheme, I mean daily life? Under Stalin – 'The hydro-electric dams are being built. Patience, there will be light, there will be water in the taps.' Under Gorbachev – 'patience! The grand reconstruction of everything is under way.' But how about . . . a pineapple?

GRISHA (*nonplussed*). This . . . endless moaning! It's our Russian cynicism, it corrodes everything . . .

LARISSA. Moaning is the sound of democracy. I begin to think that democracy is endless rows, cacophony . . .

GRISHA. Ha! Ask Boris here about 'democratic cacophony'. You want to form a new party, don't you?

BORIS (*rants*). The Communist Party of the Soviet Union is finished, Gorbachev and his gang are finished! Yeltsin is a fool. And a fool with authoritarian leanings can be dangerous. He lacks the culture of even Ligachev. There is only one reason for staying a member of the Party. To split it. Smash it from within. Our tasks are clear. We've got to build a new Socialist Party!

LARISSA. What you say could be right. But why does the way you say it, tell me it's wrong?

BORIS *ignores that.*

BORIS. Our time will come, comrades. Don't expect anything from Gorbachev. Nothing has changed for ordinary people. The liberal intelligentsia are happy. But when have they shown any fight? Fuck them. I want action. Level the lot, start again. We must form a nucleus of the SSP, the Soviet Socialist Party. I've already drafted a manifesto.

GRISHA. A party of one, Boris? Could be the start of something big. By the way my son, your accumulation of consumer goods in your flat is the envy of the entire KGB. That gleaming expresso coffee machine from Florence? That Sony 16 bit stream compact disk player? A masterpiece of the Japanese renaissance. You've got enough loot to open a special shop for the party leaders.

BORIS. You old bastard. KGB man turned Gorbachev liberal. You know why Larissa and I took you out for a meal? To tell you we're getting married next month.

LARISSA. Boris . . .

GRISHA. Well. (*He brushes his charred clothes.*) If this was the engagement party, I can't wait for the wedding.

BORIS (*under his breath*). Fuck you, Father.

LARISSA. Enough . . .

GRISHA (*low*). My son. I'm no bleeding liberal. In my veins there is still some old Bolshevik blood. What frightens me is your delusions. Don't you realise that reform communism is our last chance? Your last chance. If Gorbachev fails even the mountains will weep.

BORIS *smirks.*

You damned fool, if he's toppled, don't you know what will happen? A bloodbath. Repression. A new dictatorship. The whole country will sink.

GRISHA. And is my future daughter-in-law going to join my son's brand new movement?

LARISSA *pauses.*

LARISSA. 'Despite it all,' that's all I can say. Despite it all, I'll stay a member of the Communist Party. I don't go to the special shops, I don't cheat ten extra square metres in my flat by flashing my party card. I just . . . try to live a decent life.

BORIS. Yeah yeah, but . . .

LARISSA. The party has eighteen million members. Say three quarters are time-servers and careerists. That's five million. Write half of them off. That's still two and a half million people . . . like me.

GRISHA (*looks off*). Here's the militia.

He takes LARISSA's *glass. He raises it.*

To the marriage of two of Gorbachev's children.

He sips. Lights down on them as they go off.
Dim light on the GORBACHEVS *asleep.*
The telephone rings. GORBACHEV *switches the lamp and lifts the receiver.*

GORBACHEV. What?

A silence.

WHAT?

A silence, RAISA *stirring.*

WHAT!!!?

RAISA *sits up.*

I want a briefing in one hour's time. I will go through this *in detail.* Yes. One hour.

He slams the receiver down. He gets out of bed. He changes from his pyjamas into the GORBACHEV *clothes as the scene continues.*

RAISA. We swore, remember? . . . Swore that you would be the first
General Secretary of the Soviet Union who would *not* be on the
telephone at all hours of the night. It's a bad habit, begun by
we-know-who.

GORBACHEV. Ligachev is going to Berlin.

RAISA (*frowns*). We know Ligachev is going to Berlin. A fraternal
party visit, it's been arranged for months.

GORBACHEV. Yes! But we didn't know what he is going to say to his
fraternal comrade Erich Honecker. The boys in Dzerzhinsky
Square have just found out.

RAISA (*oddly*). The KGB never sleep.

GORBACHEV. I'm glad they do not since, for the moment, they are
on democracy's side. The intelligence report is that Ligachev will
tell Honecker privately that the Red Army will secure the GDR's
borders. That if there has to be a Tiananmen Square massacre in
the Karl Marx Allee, so be it. He'll give these guarantees in my
name! Then he'll go on what the East Germans laughably call a
television service and denounce glasnost and perestroika. I will
not have this, I will not! (*He stops dressing.*) What would Yuri
Vladimirovich Andropov have done?

RAISA. He would have had Ligachev arrested tonight, taken to a
cellar in Dzerzhinsky Square and shot.

GORBACHEV. Perhaps. Or perhaps not. (*He continues dressing.*) I
will attend the celebrations of Founder's Day in East Berlin. I will
pay my own fraternal visit to Comrade Erich Honecker.

RAISA. Tonight?

GORBACHEV. Tonight I'll think it through. As Yuri Vladimirovich
would have done.

RAISA. Right through?

He pauses. He puts his hat on.

GORBACHEV. Right through, Raisa Maximovna.

He smiles and walks off, quickly.

RAISA (*aside*). The man goes off to work, the woman is left to make
the bed. I understand this is a problem women have in the West,
too. (*She pauses.*) A politician in power works under terrible strains
but in the Soviet Union it's worse. Everything is in flux, including
power itself. That makes the pressure unbearable. Poor Misha! He

presides over the worst of bad worlds, old and new. The old will not give way gracefully like the passing year. The new will not be patient. When winter will not go and everything remains frozen, spring can be ugly, and summer . . . Summer remains a dream.

The bed goes down upon the trap. For a moment the stage is empty.
Then from one side ERICH HONECKER, *a flag sticking up out of the neck of his suit with his name on it, is helped, with considerable difficulty, up onto the table by an entourage of men in suits and large* GENERALS *in uniform. Amongst them is* EGON KRENZ, *also flagged and wearing a lower-half face-mask in a permanent big smile.*
GORBACHEV, *in coat, hat and scarf, bounds onto the table from the other side alone, and confronts them.*

HONECKER. They are all spies! Agent provocateurs! Homosexuals! Zionists!

GORBACHEV, *to the entourage.*

GORBACHEV. How much have you told him?

The entourage shuffles back a pace, with coughs and mumbles.

Have you told him eighty thousand of your citizens have fled to the West through Czechoslovakia in the last fortnight?

Coughs and mumbles from the entourage.

Well?

HONECKER. A few spies, queers, Jews.

GORBACHEV. That is what you've told him?

HONECKER. The Socialist reality of the German Democratic Republic will shine the brighter without them.

He raises a shaking finger at GORBACHEV.

I warn you, Gorbachev. The German working class decisively rejects your Moscow revisionism. The German working class will unmask your crypto-liberalism.

GORBACHEV. Tonight half a million of the German working class are on the streets, Leipzig, Dresden, East Berlin, calling for your head. (*To the entourage.*) You tell him *nothing*?

The entourage is silent.

Comrades. I have to tell you this, unequivocally. Under no circumstances whatsoever will the units of the Red Army stationed in the German Democratic Republic leave their barracks.

The entourage rustles.

KRENZ. Under no circumstances?

GORBACHEV. None.

A GENERAL. Not even against counter revolution?

GORBACHEV. Under no circumstances.

A silence, all dead still.

SECOND GENERAL. But what shall we do?

GORBACHEV (*shrugs*). Trust the people.

AN OFFICIAL. But we are the party! Therefore we are the people!
    That's what Marxism-Leninism means!

FIRST GENERAL. Moscow is abandoning us?

SECOND GENERAL. No more orders from the Soviet Union?

GORBACHEV (*smiles*). Will it be that hard for Germans to be
    without orders? All right, let me see what I can do for you. (*His
    smile goes. His gloved hand shoots a finger at* HONECKER.) This is an
    instruction from a secret session of the Politburo of the
    Communist Party of the Soviet Union. You will take the only
    possible measure to stem the flight of your citizens. You will open
    your borders to the West. There are no more strings attached.

A VOICE (*whispers*). Open the wall?

HONECKER'*s knees give way, he is caught by the two men at his side.*

HONECKER. I . . . I was a victim of fascism! I went through the
    camps! I was . . . I was true! I gave all my life . . . to the Party, to . . .
    the bright future, to . . . to the working class of the Fatherland . . .

GORBACHEV. The borders. At once.

A VOICE. But Ligachev told us . . .

GORBACHEV (*interrupts, angrily*). Comrade Ligachev is a citizen of
    the Soviet Union free to express his personal opinions.

Again, HONECKER *raises a shaky finger.*

HONECKER. I warn you.

GORBACHEV. Really? What are you going to do? Have the President
    of the USSR arrested?

HONECKER. Do not presume you are safe.

The entourage shudders, mumbles and coughs. A pause.

GORBACHEV. None of us is safe. Is personal safety important to you?

HONECKER. Because of people like you, everything socialism has gained will be lost.

GORBACHEV. Because of people like you, socialism has become a dirty word.

HONECKER. You will unleash forces no one will be able to control!

GORBACHEV. No Marxist should be afraid of the forces of history, comrade.

HONECKER *is wilting to the ground, unable to keep up.*

HONECKER. What does an upstart like you, know of history?

GORBACHEV. What do you? You froze history in your country. When the ice melts what will happen to the carcasses of the dinosaurs the cold has preserved all these years? (*To himself, looking away.*) These terrible years.

HONECKER. You . . . you will rot with us. You'll go down with us. Into the . . . (*He stutters.*) G . . . g . . . grave.

GORBACHEV (*curtly*). My conscience is clear.

He turns to go. KRENZ *steps forward and speaks, squeakily.*

KRENZ. We thank you for your fraternal remarks, comrade General Secretary.

GORBACHEV *turns and stares at* KRENZ, *who points up at his flag.*

My name is Egon Krenz.

GORBACHEV. Just do something about the mess.

GORBACHEV *walks off, quickly. The entourage carries a writhing and moaning* HONECKER *from the table and the stage.*
A rumbling sound to the opening bars of the Fourth movement of Beethoven's Ninth Symphony, very loud.
Then the Berlin Wall flies in, cutting the table in half. It is a section covered with gaudy graffiti and slogans, lit by harsh, bright light.
From the other side, people begin to tear holes in the wall, which is only paper, and clamber through onto the stage, shouting one by one . . .

CITIZENS. – I want!
  – I want!
  – I want a vote!
  – I want a decent flat!
  – I want a BMW!
  – I want to see my family!
  – I just want to look around!
  – I want!
  – I want!
  – I want to go shopping!
  – I want to read what books I like!
  – I want to hear the Berlin Philharmonic!
  – I want!
  – I want!
  – I want an elected socialist Government!
  – I want good shoes for the kids!
  – I want to get drunk in New York!
  – I want freedom!

A pause. The stage is crowded with GDR CITIZENS. Then they all shout together.

CITIZENS. WE WANT! WE WANT! WE WANT!

ACT TWO: Beyond the Wall

Scene One

GORBACHEV *alone at the centre of the huge table, a cup of coffee in his hand.*

GORBACHEV. Come then, don't hold back. All out in the open. Misfortunes. Pains. Indignations. Passions. Hopes, Loves. Hates. Illusions. Fears. Truth is concrete apprehension of reality.

GORBACHEV sips his cup of coffee and walks away.
A trap opens and ZOYA, KATYA and LENA come up out of the trap with a banner on two poles. It reads 'PERESTROIKA'. They set it up at the back of the table and stand it in a huddle.
LENIN *walks up out of the trap. He takes up a position near the back of the table. He adopts the pose of a statue.*
A Leningrad rock group, a trio, skinheads with swastikas painted on their foreheads comes up out of the trap onto the table top. Their lead guitarist is playing appallingly, with feedback through a small speaker carried by the second rocker. The third rocker carries a stuffed pigeon. He goes and puts the stuffed pigeon – some kind of device to secure it – on LENIN's head.
Then, following the Leningrad band one by one, come groups from all over the Soviet Union. In contrast to the 1917 pageant at the beginning of Act One, the 'PERESTROIKA pageant' is chaotic, unfocused, bad tempered. They take up positions on the stage with their banners, national flags and placards, as if the table top were a market place. The rock band plays intermittently . . .
Two Azerbaijan MUSLIMS, *one with a green headband, one with a red headband. They chant, overlapping each other . . .*

RED HEADBAND. There is only one God and Mohammed is his prophet . . .

GREEN HEADBAND. There is only one God and Mohammed is his prophet . . .

RED HEADBAND. There is only one . . .

They continue to chant.
Next two RUSSIAN FASCISTS *come up, carrying a banner which reads:*
THE JEWS KILLED OUR TSAR. *They carry a mock coffin, upon it the slogan*
RUSSIA 1917-90: KILLED BY THE JEWS. *They have a petition which is on one*
continuous lavatory-type roll, which they invite ZOYA, KATYA *and*
LENA *to sign.*

1ST RUSSIAN FASCIST. Russia for the Russians!

2ND RUSSIAN FASCIST. Free Russia from the Jews!

1ST RUSSIAN FASCIST. The Jews are poisoning Russia with vodka!

2ND RUSSIAN FASCIST. Sign the petition against the Jews!

The three WOMEN *shake their heads.*
And next come a BALTIC MAN *and three* BALTIC WOMEN *in*
national costumes, dancing, each with their National flag. They sing, in
exquisite folk-song harmony.

BALTIC FOLKLORISTS. We used to be so happy
　　Happy proud and free.
　　'Til Stalin talked to Hitler
　　And stole our countries three –
　　Now our flags fly high again
　　Oh please oh please oh please
　　Don't let it be in vain.

And they are drowned by the Leningrad rock group who screech a punk
song.

Freedom is a load of piss
I don't see no way out of this
(*Chorus.*) Fucked fucked fucked
Fucked in Leningrad
Fucked fucked fucked
With all the shit I've had
Fuck fuck fuck
Fucked in Leningrad.

The band disintegrates into a wail of feedback.

Next come the MOSCOW MAFIA, *led by a godfather figure who carries a*
machine gun and two other GANGSTERS. *One carries a placard which*
reads MOSCOW MAFIA: FIRST COME FIRST SERVED, *the other carries a number*
of ghetto blasters; he barks his wares.

2ND GANGSTER. Sony, Sony, Sony Panasonic! Here we go folks, hard currency only! Sony, Sony, Sony Panasonic!

Next come two ARMENIANS, *victims of the Armenian earthquake, on crutches and in filthy bandages, with begging bowls. They carry a placard which reads* ARMENIA.
Then, pushing past the ARMENIANS, *come the conservatives represented by* LIGACHEV, ZAIKOV, VICTOR (*ex-editor of 'Pravda'*) *and the 'Rosa Kleb' figure of* RIMMA ZHUKOVA. *They carry with them a red banner in the old iconography, Marx's, Lenin's and Stalin's profiles upon it and the slogan 'BRING BACK THE OLD DAYS'.*
LIGACHEV *tries to distribute sweets to* ZOYA, KATYA *and* LENA, *a ghastly smile on his face.*

LIGACHEV. Sweeties? Sweeties? Anyone? Ladies? Real Marxism Leninism?

ZOYA, KATYA and LENA recoil.
BORIS YELTSIN *rises from the trap. He is slightly drunk and dishevelled and is holding a bunch of flowers in each hand. He waltzes up to* LENA *in the distance and then goes down on one knee and offers her first one bunch and then the other. She is embarrassed but accepts them. Finally come two* MINERS *in pit helmets, their faces unwashed. They carry two placards. The first placard reads* LENIN 1917: LAND, PEACE, BREAD, *the second reads* 1990: SOAP, FOOD, FREEDOM.
A perestroika market place . . . they sing, dance, shout, ply their wares in a cacophony.
GORBACHEV *moves.*
At once, everyone is still but for the two MUSLIMS. *He turns to them.*

RED HEADBAND. Gorbachev! Common European home, what does that mean to the Muslims of the South?

GREEN HEADBAND. We're Asians, not Europeans. Our common home is Iran, Afghanistan . . .

RED HEADBAND. We'll smash our way out of your 'common home' . . .

GREEN HEADBAND. Out of the house of the infidel . . .

The BALTIC FOLKLORISTS *come to life.* GORBACHEV *turns to them.*

1ST BALTIC WOMAN. We've had enough of you Russians! . . .

2ND BALTIC WOMAN. Gorbachev! You don't understand why we Lithuanians, Latvians, Estonians want our freedom. It's because all you Russians are of mixed blood! . . .

BALTIC MAN. Nothing pure about you! Tartars and Mongols invaded your villages, raped your women and left their mark on you forever. Just look at your own wife . . .

GORBACHEV *recoils, turns on his heel to the two* MUSLIMS.

GREEN HEADBAND. You can never win . . .

RED HEADBAND. Grasshoppers . . .

GREEN HEADBAND. Have you seen how grasshoppers cross a river? The first goes down to the bank and is carried away by the water, then a second comes, a third . . .

RED HEADBAND. Hundreds, thousands . . .

GREEN HEADBAND. And their dead bodies rise above the water, a bridge . . . and the other grasshoppers cross safely.

RED HEADBAND. We've learnt more from these grasshoppers than we have from you Russians.

GORBACHEV. Every . . . (*He pauses, shaken.*) Everything is negotiable. Just stop the killing. Let the trains go into Armenia. You are human beings, not grasshoppers.

The BALTIC WOMEN *come to life again.* GORBACHEV *turns to them.*

BALTIC MAN. Every Russian is mixed. A hotch-potch.

1ST BALTIC WOMAN. That's why Russians are so aggressive. It's the only way you can prove yourselves.

2ND BALTIC WOMAN. Gorbachev, take the Russians. Byelorussians and Ukrainians back to Russia. Get them out.

A BALTIC MAN *steps up onto the table, unseen, behind the* BALTIC FOLKLORISTS *and pushes in front of them.*

BALTIC MAN. Don't listen to her! She doesn't speak for us. Suddenly there are lunatics in national costumes everywhere. This racist gibberish doesn't speak for everyone. You must believe that.

GORBACHEV. I do. (*To the* FOLKLORISTS.) I appeal to you, I beg you. Remember: the struggle for purity always ends badly for the pure!

The FOLKLORISTS *pull the* THIRD BALTIC WOMAN *back behind them and hiss at* GORBACHEV.

He turns to the conservatives. They step backwards, but a young woman
TEACHER, *in severe glasses, steps up onto the table unseen and pushes*
her way through them. She takes two steps forward with military precision
and shouts at GORBACHEV.

TEACHER. I cannot. I am a teacher. I will not betray my principles.

GORBACHEV. What are they?

TEACHER. The foundations of our state. Built by them. (*She points*
to the iconograph of the three profiles of MARX, LENIN *and* STALIN.)

GORBACHEV. The first never saw our state. The second died,
agonizing over the problems of our state. The third was a
murderer of our people, a scoundrel and peasant-slayer.

The conservatives hiss at GORBACHEV.

TEACHER. I do not agree. He led us during the war. Our press tells
lies. My pupils now question everything. There is no more
discipline. No law and order. The cosmopolitans are being
rehabilitated. I tell you I cannot and will not betray my principles.

GORBACHEV. What do you teach?

TEACHER. Chemistry.

GORBACHEV. Not history. (*A pause.*) What is the formula for
water?

TEACHER. H_2O . . .

GORBACHEV. But suppose someone has been telling our people
for fifty years that the formula for water was really H_2SO_4,
sulphuric acid. What would you say?

TEACHER. Send him to a psychiatric clinic.

GORBACHEV. Don't worry. Nobody will do that to you. Think
again, Comrade.

GORBACHEV *turns to the* MINERS. *The rock group wave to him.*

ROCKER. Hey Gorby man! We want a contract with EMI. Can you
perestroik us a deal, man?

GORBACHEV. Get that obscenity off your skulls.

The rock band shuffles uneasily.

(*To one of the* MINERS.) How old are you?

1ST MINER. Twenty-seven, comrade Gorbachev. And a member of the Party since '85. I joined when you became General Secretary.

GORBACHEV. Good. But why are you on strike?

2ND MINER (*sarcastically*). Soap? The Russians love a religious mystery! Like Jesus going up to heaven, into thin air. It's no mystery. All the soap's been carted off by the apparatus villains and sold to line their filthy pockets. (*He gives a strange laugh.*) A worker's state where the workers have no soap because it's been stolen by the very people who say we're a workers' state!

GORBACHEV. The local party informs me that hotheads have taken over your strike committee.

1ST MINER. Hotheads? Do you know who's on our strike committee? A cutter-loader operator, a mine director, an electrician and party committee member, a tunneller, a trade union committee chairman, a very lively woman lamp room attendant and the organisation secretary of the Young Communist League . . .

2ND MINER. The vanguard of the working class? That crap phrase of the party hacks? You want the vanguard?

1ST MINER. Here we are, comrade.

2ND MINER. Where's the plunder from our workdays gone, Gorbachev? It's not just soap. It's life itself. Where's any life at all for us, Gorbachev?

1ST MINER. That's why we cabled you to come and see us.

GORBACHEV *pauses. Then he speaks, fast. Decisive gestures with his arm.*

GORBACHEV. What you say is indisputable. Your demands are just. Your anger is understandable. We will move fast and meet all your demands, including democracy.

A pause. The MINERS *stare at him, sullenly.*

1ST MINER. But that's what the local party said when we went on strike last spring. They gave us everything then . . .

GORBACHEV (*rapping his sentences out*). All I ask is for a little more patience. I know I know, but I still ask and I will come and ask all those who have elected you the same. The past was ugly. The present is unbearable. The future is all.

He turns on his heel, walks a few paces, staring into his cup of coffee. As the MINERS *speak their increasingly angry chant, the rest of the perestroika pageant stirs into life with increasing cacophony.*

IST MINER. For years we were told . . .

2ND MINER. . . . produce more coal.

1ST MINER. Don't worry about a thing . . .

2ND MINER. . . . We'll give you all the food you can eat . . .

1ST MINER. . . . the drink you can drink . . . new clothes so you don't stink . .

2ND MINER. Model workers flats and . . .

1ST MINER *and* 2ND MINER. K-i-n-d-e-r-g-a-r-t-e-n-s!

1ST MINER. Free holidays, palaces of culture . . .

2ND MINER. And lots and lots . . .

1ST MINER. Lots and lots of sport . . .

2ND MINER. Lots and lots . . .

1ST MINER. Of nothing at all.

The cacophony rising. The MINERS *straining to make themselves heard.*

Now it's 'going on strike?' . . .

2ND MINER. 'Strike? Leave your party cards behind' . . .

1ST MINER. Say the apparatchiks . . .

2ND MINER. . . . the party hacks . . .

1ST MINER. Having trampled on us for years by virtue of their position in our Party . . . and now they laugh at us . . .

2ND MINER. . . . 'Don't just produce coal . . .

1ST MINER. . . . produce everything for yourselves' . . .

2ND MINER. Let them be warned, we can, we will . . .

1ST MINER. We will work days and nights . . .

2ND MINER. . . . work for ourselves and others like us . . .

1ST MINER. But not for the parasites not any more.

2ND MINER. Not any more.

> YELTSIN *applauds the* MINERS' *chant. Fighting and shoving,*
> *shouting, the Leningrad group screeching its punk song, the*
> FOLKLORISTS *spitting out their folksong, the two* MUSLIMS *waving*
> *knives, the Mafia* GODFATHER *threatening with his machine gun, the*
> *pageant becomes a morass in uproar.* YELTSIN *joins the cacophony and is*
> *clearly singing, but it is impossible to hear a single word. Then as they*
> *realise that* YELTSIN *is performing there is a gradual quiet. When*
> *everyone is silent* YELTSIN *walks up to* GORBACHEV *and sings. All*
> *except* GORBACHEV *join the chorus.*
> YELTSIN *sings, to 'The Volga Boatmen.'*

YELTSIN. One thing we know
(*Chorus.*)
One thing we know
You have lost your glow
(*Chorus.*)
You have lost your glow

One thing we know
Perestroika is too slow
(*Chorus.*)
One thing we know
Perestroika is too slow

We know who's holding it back
Let's give them all the sack
(*Chorus.*)
Let's give them all the sack

But of one thing beware
The people they do shout
Mikhail Sergeyevich
If you don't agree with us
You're out.

(*Chorus.*)
Mikhail Sergeyevich
If you don't agree with us
You're out.

> *Loud cheers and applause.* YELTSIN *goes off.* GORBACHEV *is silent,*
> *stony-faced. Suddenly a* VOICE *is heard in the crowd. All, for a moment,*
> *are still.*

A VOICE. Beef fat! In the supermarket at the end of Arbut Street!
They are selling beef fat!

At once a stampede as everyone is pulling out nylon shopping bags and fighting to form a queue. In one knot fists fly. In contrast to the sullen queues of Act One, this queue is bad-tempered, jostling. GORBACHEV walks forward from it, with his cup of coffee.

CITIZENS in the crowd, turning to each other. ZOYA, KATYA and LENA stand at the end of the queue.

1ST CITIZEN. Hurry up! Or the Jews will have got it all!

2ND. They say the fucking yids have eaten it all!

4TH. Not the Jews, they've all run away to Israel. It'll be the fucking Bolsheviks.

5TH. The fucking Bolsheviks have eaten it all.

6TH. Have you heard that Raisa, our Tsarina, has a new lover?

MANY. *Who?*

6TH. A failed architect from Latvia! He's building them a special dacha in Sukhumi.

7TH. You know Gorbachev's grandfather was a Muslim?

8TH. Oi you!

9TH. What?

8TH. Are you a Georgian?

KATYA. When did we begin to abuse each other in the Moscow queues? Suddenly it's begun.

10TH. There's a Georgian in this queue!

LENA. It's a question of when do you actually begin starving? Are we starving now? Is this it? How many days ago did you drink milk, Katya?

9TH. I'm not from Georgia!

11TH. There's scum from Georgia here!

ZOYA (*aside*). Compassion.

12TH. Georgian scum! Fuck off back home! Get out of Moscow. Can't you see there's not enough food for us here?

ZOYA (*aside*). Consolation. Hope and patience. All are going together.

The queue becomes out of hand, people pushing each other to the ground. A trap opens and they spill down into it. The last opens an empty shopping

bag and holds it, open and empty, to GORBACHEV, *like a begging bowl.*
GORBACHEV *shakes his head. The* SHOPPER *makes an angry gesture
at him and scuttles down the trap.*
Silence. GORBACHEV *remains standing still, looking into his cup of
coffee.* CHERNOBYL MAN *wanders onto the stage, humming 'Ring a
ring o' roses'. He is heavily sun-tanned. He wears country clothes, shabby,
with loose, dirty trousers and mud-stained boots.* GORBACHEV *stares at
him, transfixed.* CHERNOBYL MAN *circles* GORBACHEV. *He recites,
very softly.*

CHERNOBYL MAN. Ring a ring o' roses, pocket full o' posies, it's
blown up, it's blown up, we all fall down. Why do the houses glow
like candles at night? All fall . . .

He drops to the floor and stares at the audience. GORBACHEV *rushes up
to him. Hearing a noise the man jumps up to his feet at attention.*

CHERNOBYL MAN. Comrade! Are you alright?

He holds out his hand. CHERNOBYL MAN *steps back.*

CHERNOBYL MAN. Move back, Mikhail Sergeyevich! Move back!
Can't you see I'm dripping radiation, head to foot?

GORBACHEV (*withdrawing his hand slowly. A whisper*). Who are you?

CHERNOBYL MAN (*sing-song*). I am a man from the country of
horses with five legs, pigs with two heads, and human babies with
six toes . . . (*He stops that. A fake heartiness.*) I'm sorry. I'm Chernobyl
man. One of the liquidators, comrade. Sent by Moscow to
liquidate the crisis after the reactor exploded . . . I ran! A
handkerchief tied over my mouth! Thirty seconds a time, on the
broken wall of the reactor! To throw a bag of cement! I . . .

For a moment he is silent, transfixed. GORBACHEV *shuts his eyes.*
CHERNOBYL MAN *changes note again and sounds broken.*

I came back to Moscow, like this. My wife and children wept but
asked me to leave the house. The risk was too great. Radiation is
infectious, they said. That's why they've sealed off a whole
cemetery in Moscow, where some of the victims were buried. The
whole cemetery is radioactive. Did you know?

GORBACHEV. Where do you live now?

CHERNOBYL MAN *roars with laughter.*

CHERNOBYL MAN. What a sweet question! I have gone back to the
contaminated zone. The dead zone. No problems at all, Mikhail
Sergeyevich. Plenty of unoccupied houses.

GORBACHEV. And food?

CHERNOBYL MAN. Food?

CHERNOBYL MAN *laughs.*

What's the problem? I have an amazing kitchen garden. Tomatoes as big as your head. Cucumbers the size of Boris Yeltsin. Mushrooms! Ah the mushrooms, a real treat for my Sunday lunches. Don't be upset. At least I live in peace. Nobody to harass me. My life is quiet and I'll die in peace. Sleep well, Mikhail Sergeyevich. I won't live to see it, but I hope you win.

He goes off. GORBACHEV *sits on the edge of the table, his back bowed, his coffee beside him.* ZOYA, KATYA *and* LENA *take the perestroika banner down.*

ZOYA. Do you know what I think our country's like nowadays? A giant food freezer.

LENA. A food freezer. Will I ever have one of those?

KATYA. The Soviet Union is like a giant food freezer . . .

ZOYA. Stuffed full of things.

KATYA *shakes her head.*

Don't get it.

ZOYA. All kinds of things that have been frozen for fifty years. But now it's broken down! Don't you see? It's unfrozen! And everything in it . . . is rotting! Stinking! Unfit for human consumption!

LENA *shrugs.*

LENA. I see what you mean.

They go off down the trap. LENIN, *as a statue, pigeon on his head, remains at the back of the table.* GORBACHEV *walks to the front and puts his cup of coffee on the edge, then sits, his legs dangling over the edge. He rubs his hands over his face and lifts his coffee cup.*
A light change.
Dramatic red light on the LENIN *'statue'. Flickering light. An effect like a poor video film, flicking, black and white with odd blotches of colour.*
President CEAUŞESCU *of Romania and his wife* ELENA *come on. They are dressed as they were seen on the video of their trial.*

CEAUŞESCU. I do not recognise this court. My name is Nikolai Ceauşescu. I am President of the Romanian Republic, I will answer only to the Romanian People's Assembly and to the working class. This is an armed coup, engineered by terrorists and the foreign enemies of Romania. You are coupists. (*The single touch to his wife's hand.*) The people had everything they needed! You are Bonapartists and terrorists! I do not recognise this court!

Six Romanian SOLDIERS *march, with goose steps, onto the stage. A firing squad. They fire. The* CEAUŞESCUS *fall across each other. The* SOLDIERS *cross themselves and march off . . . as* LIGACHEV, ZAIKOV *and* VICTOR *come up onto the table.*
The bodies of the CEAUŞESCUS *remain there.*
The light on LENIN *changes.*

Scene Two

GORBACHEV *sitting on the edge of the table. He has not drunk his coffee.* LENIN, *in statue pose with the pigeon on his head, remains at the back, still immobile.*
A trap door opens. YAKOVLEV *hurries up on the stage, a sheaf of telexes in his hand. He is tense. He looks around and sees* GORBACHEV. *He stands still.*

GORBACHEV (*to himself*). Why is our destiny so impenetrable? The *point* of government is to know what you are doing! To do that, you need to know what will happen. That is why history must be a science, it must! If it is not, how can we foresee the consequences of our actions? How is government possible?

YAKOVLEV. Mikhail Sergeyevich . . . What are you doing?

GORBACHEV. Sitting in this window. I wonder, why are there so many window seats in these Kremlin apartments?

YAKOVLEV. Perhaps the Tsars had nothing to do but sit around all day.

GORBACHEV *snaps at him.*

GORBACHEV. The Praesidium has adjourned for half an hour, comrade Yakovlev. I am not wasting my time.

YAKOVLEV. No, comrade General Secretary.

A pause.

GORBACHEV. How many will die if we do it?

YAKOVLEV (*waving the telexes*). The telexes are very bad, they are killing each other in the South, there's no doubt. It's a pogrom.

GORBACHEV. I asked you – how many will die if we do this thing?

YAKOVLEV *pauses*.

YAKOVLEV. Do you want a party hack's answer? 'No one will die, comrade General Secretary! The people of the Republic of Azerbaijan will welcome the Red Army with flowers!'

GORBACHEV. Yes, that's what Yazov says.

YAKOVLEV. Do you want a realistic answer? Four hundred deaths. Do you want a friend's answer?

GORBACHEV. No. Yes.

YAKOVLEV. Don't do it. The party conservatives are 'bum rapping you'.

GORBACHEV. I believe the phrase is 'giving me a bum rap'.

YAKOVLEV. Ligachev's friends in Baku want you to be blamed for a massacre. As they did in Tiblisi.

GORBACHEV. Tiblisi. Thirty-eight dead.

YAKOVLEV (*gushing*). You were not at the meeting of the Praesidium that ordered the troops to Tiblisi. Comrade Ligachev was in the chair, that's well known, you're not blamed for what happened . . .

GORBACHEV. No? But I am in the chair tonight! (*To himself.*) Meetings at night, ordering massacres. Are we going down that path? (*To* YAKOVLEV.) The special troops flown into Tiblisi had little silver spades, to slash the demonstrators. Did I know there were Red Army troops, specially trained to cut people down with little silver spades? I did not, I did not. Did you?

YAKOVLEV *shakes his head once, looking down.* GORBACHEV *shouts.*

What kind of mind conceived of such a thing? Those spades may yet have cost the Soviet Union Georgia! (*Lower.*) You think I'm rambling.

YAKOVLEV. No, no Mikhail Sergeyevich . . .

GORBACHEV. It's having to knock heads together so often in the

Supreme Soviet on television, shouting. Tell me not to.

YAKOVLEV. Do not shout on television.

> GORBACHEV *looks around at* YAKOVLEV. *They laugh.*
> GORBACHEV *looks forward, his smile gone.*

GORBACHEV (*to himself*). Four hundred deaths? But that's not real, that's just an anticipation, a fear, will that happen or not? Either way who will die, who will be saved? How do we make the judgement? What is the science of it?

> YAKOVLEV *looks at his watch.*

GORBACHEV (*as if he has seen him do so*). Fifteen minutes.

YAKOVLEV. But what shall we do?

GORBACHEV. Have a cup of coffee.

YAKOVLEV. If we order Yazov to send the Red Army into Azerbaijan we could catch the British disease, called Ulster? And bleed for twenty years . . .

> *A helpless gesture.*

For the Soviet Union it could be fatal.

GORBACHEV. Have a cup of coffee, citizen!

> YAKOVLEV *looks at him for a moment, then goes off quickly down the trap.*
> GORBACHEV *takes a sip of coffee.*
> Then LENIN *takes the pigeon off his head and looks at it.*

LENIN. What an internationalist proletarian bird the pigeon is. Present in every country in the world, shitting on every leader's head.

> *He puts the pigeon under his arm and his hands in his pockets, in the characteristic pose.*
> Then ANDROPOV *walks up onto the table from the trap. He walks about, relaxed and smoking a cigarette, blowing clouds of smoke, Russian style. Through the scene* LENIN *and* ANDROPOV *do not look at each other.*

LENIN. The dialectic of partial conquests!

GORBACHEV (*startled*). What?

ANDROPOV. An interesting formulation.

LENIN. Every bureaucratic apparatus is guided by this dialectic. It makes them conservative. Moving forward is always a risk because they worry they will lose what they've already got. No foolish leaps in the dark for them. It's the dialectics of fools. Risks are necessary. I took one in 1917.

GORBACHEV. I know. That's what worries me. The well of socialism is drying up, Vladimir Ilyich.

LENIN *chuckles.*

GORBACHEV. If I order troops to Azerbaijan, I do not know . . . if my conscience will be clear.

LENIN. Yes that's a rule of thumb of yours, 'conscience'.

ANDROPOV. Yes, Cromwell used to say something similar, about 'being right in the bowels of Christ'.

LENIN. I suppose as a rule of thumb, 'conscience' does as well as any other. But as a policy, Mikhail Sergeyevich? As a programme of socialist renewal?

GORBACHEV. What else can people understand? What else can they respect?

LENIN. Pfft. Pigeon shit is dripping off your shoulders too. They love you in the West, but at home they're moaning.

ANDROPOV. Not a good word to say for you.

GORBACHEV. Popularity is not the point.

LENIN. Correct.

ANDROPOV. Correct.

LENIN. Who was that fool in the Praesidium who said that 'The borders of the Soviet Union are the holiest of the holies'?

GORBACHEV. Ligachev.

LENIN. 'Holiest of the holiest?' A border? What is this Slav nationalist cant? I would never have said such a thing, never!

ANDROPOV *puffs his cigarette.*

ANDROPOV. So, Misha, you are not only to be the Soviet Cromwell, banging heads together in the Supreme Soviet, and in the streets of every Lithuanian town, but now you are to be our Abraham Lincoln, sending troops south to save the Union?

GORBACHEV. Yuri Vladimorovich. Did you foresee these difficulties?

ANDROPOV. No. Did you?

GORBACHEV. No. (*He points at* LENIN.) Did he?

ANDROPOV *shrugs and walks.*

LENIN. Pfft, the business of good government. Muck and shit. What was the First World War, but a well, poisoned by a billion tons of muck and shit? That's what we inherited in October '17. *Everything* poisoned. Then the well of Soviet socialism itself was contaminated. Don't winge, Mikhail Sergeyevich! (*He walks to the trap.*) Buy time! Impossible to leap over the world market. A deal with the Germans is vital to revive the economy and your hopes. Do it, but without any illusions. I see them as vultures once again, ready to swoop. Poland is bad for profits, leave it alone, Prague is good for profits, capture the market. Did you read the *Financial Times* today?

GORBACHEV. No.

LENIN. For the first time the Frankfurt Stock Exchange overtook London. Now do you understand?

GORBACHEV. No, no Vladimir Ilyich.

LENIN. East and West, socialism, capitalism, both are unstable. Buy time. The world is yet to be made. (*He raises his hand, a wave of salute.*) I envy you.

ANDROPOV *offers* LENIN *a cigarette from a cigarette case.* LENIN *waves it aside.*

LENIN. Only the occasional cheroot. (*To* GORBACHEV.) My mummified corpse is still at the Kremlin wall! Do something about it! Before rioters kick me into dust, all over Red Square, singing 'God save the Tsar'.

He walks down into the trap quickly, out of sight.
YAKOVLEV *hurries back on, the telexes in his hand.* ANDROPOV *takes them and flicks through them.* YAKOVLEV *does not notice.*

ANDROPOV. Your problem is . . . how good is the information you receive? How *real* are these reports? The Azerbaijan National Front is preparing an uprising. But is it? Or is this about corrupt apparatchiks, frightened sick. Fearful of losing power and patronage. Stirring up nationalist hatreds to win a new legitimacy by killing Armenians in Baku. Something a good police force

could handle by locking a couple of dozen people up on a
Saturday night and punching a few faces. You don't know.

He puts the telexes back in YAKOVLEV's *hands.* YAKOVLEV *walks
away, reading one of them.*

ANDROPOV (*a wave of the hand*). Anarchy and pogrom, genocide
in the making . . . Or village feuds a thousand years old, getting
out of hand? Which?

GORBACHEV. The party cannot let go yet, it cannot.

ANDROPOV. It's party apparatchiks who are plotting against you in
Baku. Being nationalist, to save their own skins . . .

GORBACHEV (*muttering*). Cannot, cannot yet. The centre must
hold, how can we reform, remould . . . if everything falls apart in
our hands? (*To* ANDROPOV.) I wonder what you would have
done.

ANDROPOV. Crushed them. (*He smiles.*) I told you once that I was
a primitive man, I had to be, I lived in primitive times. Have times
changed? (*He raises a hand, cigarette between his fingers.*) I don't
envy you at all.

ANDROPOV *goes off, down the trap.* GORBACHEV *turns to*
YAKOVLEV.

GORBACHEV. I will sign the order.

YAKOVLEV *stares at him for a moment.*

YAKOVLEV. But . . .

GORBACHEV *whirls round at him in a rage.*

GORBACHEV. What? What did you say? What?

YAKOVLEV. Nothing, comrade President.

YAKOVLEV *goes off.* GORBACHEV *is about to follow him but stops
and speaks aside.*

GORBACHEV. Sixty years. Sixty years the leaders have been staring
at something lying there. In the shit. Barely recognisable. They've
not dared to look at it, they've rushed by. Clean the square for
the big parade! They never asked, what is that thing, lying there
in the shit? They never asked because they knew that the thing
lying there, in the shit, is the people. Our people. (*Muttering to
himself.*) And as if that is not enough, as if that is not enough . . .
(*He collects himself and continues.*) As if that wasn't enough, in the

first year of perestroika, the reactor blew. Eight hundred
thousand children are suffering from leukaemia, four million
people are living in a contaminated area . . . Glasnost? Openness?
How can a leader of this country bring himself to tell . . . four
million of his people that they are doomed? That their children's
children's children are already condemned? What leader of a
country has ever had to do that, I . . . (*He pauses. He controls
himself.*) On one level things have never been better, and because
they've never been better the people are free to say they've never
been worse. (*Muttering to himself.*) But, the econ, econ, economy
. . (*And sharply.*) A command economy. As a child, I thought it to
be a wonder of the world. I lose a button on my school coat.
Somewhere in one of thirty-six ministries for planning, someone
has calculated how many school boys will lose buttons, on how
many school coats, and an order has gone to the button factory
'So many, no more no less'. And there are buttons for all. Except.
Except for the one third of buttons that only exist on paper, and
another third that have been siphoned off for the black market,
so the button factory manager can make a few roubles on the
side, build a dacha and run a mistress in Moscow . . . It should
work, but it demonstrably does not, the Utopia of buttons
produces . . . children with ragged school coats. (*Angrily.*) To
attempt to govern this country, is like trying to teach a penguin to
fly! (*He pauses. Then chuckles at that thought.*) The trick is to devise
a socialism that human nature can handle. Which means . . . (*He
smiles to himself.*) One of the most powerful men on earth, the
General Secretary of the Communist Party of the Soviet Union,
accumulating enormous power to give it away. And what leader of
a country has ever done that? Given the power away to that thing,
lying in the corner, in the shit. (*He braces himself.*) Meanwhile the
pogroms in Azerbaijan must be stopped.

The bodies of the CEAUŞESCUS *still lie there.*
LIGACHEV *and* ZAIKOV *come on and meet* VICTOR, *the ex-editor of*
Pravda. *They are excited, embracing each other, slapping each other on
the back, shaking hands.*

LIGACHEV. That's it comrades! He's done for himself!

ZAIKOV. He signed the order. In the name of all that is holy in
Russia, he signed the order!

LIGACHEV. I always knew it. The man's a namby-pamby crypto
liberal, out of his depth.

ZAIKOV. They'll be nailing pictures of him up in Baku! Blood smeared on his mouth . . .

LIGACHEV. That's what we need! 'Gorbachev, slayer of innocents!'

They laugh.

(*To* VICTOR.) Well Vitya? I told you didn't I? The Balkans will come to our aid. The old tinder box of Europe will burn this perestroika down.

VICTOR. If only I was still editing *Pravda*.

LIGACHEV. You will again, you will.

VICTOR. Then I could tell the truth.

LIGACHEV (*a sweep of his hand*). 'Gorbachev slayer of innocents'.

VICTOR. Yes, I was thinking of a more popular format. (*Angrily.*) *Pravda*'s so bloody wet these days, you need an umbrella to read it. People are being misled by ersatz newspapers, like *Moscow News*.

ZAIKOV. News? It's horse-shit!

LIGACHEV. All the rags of glasnost . . .

VICTOR. Ogonyok?

ZAIKOV. Cowdung!

VICTOR. *Ndelya*, the so-called supplement to *Izvestia*?

ZAIKOV. The excretions of an elephant with stomach trouble.

LIGACHEV. *Fakti i Argumenti*?

ZAIKOV. Untreated sewage.

VICTOR. Written by rats for sewer rats.

They laugh. LIGACHEV *embraces them.*

LIGACHEV. It's nice to be with friends again. Let's celebrate! We'll cut the balls off this 'Gorb', this country bumpkin from out of town. We'll tie him up tight in a straight-jacket called Azerbaijan. He'll squirm now, shouting about 'democracy' . . . but he'll never break free. Comrades! The old guard will have its day again.

RIMA ZHUKOVA *in her 'Rosa Kleb' outfit, comes on quickly.*

ZAIKOV. Rimma, my angel!

VICTOR (*low*). Avenging angel.

RIMMA. What are you all so happy about? Blood on the streets of Baku?

ZAIKOV. Isn't it wonderful news?

RIMMA. Don't be deceived by Azerbaijan. That strengthens him. He'll be seen as a no nonsense leader. And our faction still has some friends in Dzerzhinsky Square.

LIGACHEV. What are they saying?

RIMMA. That he plans to bypass the party.

ZAIKOV. What?

VICTOR. Bypass the party. In *this* country?

CEAUŞESCU's corpse raises its head.

CEAUŞESCU. Psst, you. Psst.

A pause.

LIGACHEV. Who spoke?

CEAUŞESCU. Over here, you idiots.

They turn.

LIGACHEV. Comrade Ceauşescu! I thought you were dead.

CEAUŞESCU. Comrade Ligachev, surely you must know old Stalinists never die. We are reborn somewhere else. Hello there, comrade Rimma. I could have done with someone like you in Bucharest. (*He laughs. Then his face freezes.*) Listen, listen. Gorbachev is plotting. The man with the steel teeth, isn't that what your Gromyko called him? I warn you. Look at me, I thought I had scoured my country clean of his kind, scoured everywhere with acid, with terror. Then suddenly there were thousands. He will get rid of all of you. You will be sent down like me. Unless.

ZAIKOV. Unless. (*To* CEAUŞESCU.) Long live the dictatorship of the proletariat! Long live Marxism-Leninism!

CEAUŞESCU gives a characteristic, jerky wave of his arm, and subsides.

LIGACHEV. Comrades. We are faced with anarchy.

VICTOR. The loss of our jobs.

LIGACHEV. Anarchy! Reaction! Disorder!

A pause.

We must talk to the Red Army.

They hurry off, in a huddle, LIGACHEV *giving unheard instructions.*

Scene Three

GORBACHEV *comes on, shoulders rounded, and stumbles to the centre of the table. He rotates an arm slowly, feeling his shoulder. He slowly undresses. A massage table rises on a trap, at its foot three bottles of oil and towels. He wraps a towel around himself and levers himself, exhausted, onto the table face down.*
RAISA *comes on. She is wearing a dirty pink designer track suit.*

RAISA. Oil?

GORBACHEV. Please, Raya Maximovna. I don't want to discuss the Middle East.

RAISA. I mean which oil do you want me to rub on your body?

GORBACHEV. Ah. Er. Sorry. I think . . . the almond oil.

RAISA *takes a bottle and begins the massage. As she is rubbing his shoulders and spine she talks in rhythm to the movements of the massage.*

RAISA. Incubus . . . Incubus . . . Incubus . . .

GORBACHEV (*drowsily*). What . . . ?

RAISA. All those years I taught philosophy at the University. Only now, I think I understand what he meant. Marx. Incubus. He uses the word often, you know. The weight of the dead generations oppressing the living, like an incubus. We know what that means, my tired, my exhausted Misha. Shoulder blades jammed, weighted under the incubus. Oh! Can you feel it? Your body is full of knots. Relax, it hurts my fingers. Ah, here's Azerbaijan.

She rubs his shoulders going down slowly.

And Georgia. There. There. (*As she approaches his bum.*) And here are the Baltic republics. (*Massaging his bum cheeks.*) So you want independence, eh? Where would that leave him?

GORBACHEV, *amused despite himself.*

GORBACHEV. Raya! How can I relax with your non-stop politics and philosophy. Enough!

RAISA *laughs.*

RAISA. If you turn over, I'll massage Yeltsin for you.

GORBACHEV *looks at her. Then laughs and relaxes as she continues to massage his back.*

Shall I tell you a story of the old days?

GORBACHEV. Hmmm.

RAISA. You know the Potemkin story?

GORBACHEV. Of course I know the damn Potemkin story. How many times have we seen the film? (*Mumbling.*) Marx, Eisenstein .. what other head of state gets rubbed down with philosophy and culture?

RAISA. You don't know the Potemkin story.

GORBACHEV *groans.*

Shh! The battleship was named after the Chancellor of Empress Catherine. Did you know that?

GORBACHEV. Yes!

RAISA. You didn't!

GORBACHEV. Right, I didn't!

RAISA. Good. (*The story is mimed by* RAISA, *who plays Catherine in Thatcherite tones.*) There was once a great Empress, Catherine. She had a Chancellor, a great favourite, whose name was Potemkin. He was totally loyal and the only person who could tell her unpleasant truths.

GORBACHEV *sits up.*

Then, one day he tells her that her latest lover is wreaking havoc amongst the nobility. He wants her to give up the young man. She explodes with anger. 'Potemkin you go too far. I will not tolerate this.' He bows and retires. And . . . the cares of state begin to tell on Potemkin. He suffers from bouts of depression. The nobles complain, but Catherine hates any reference to her Chancellor's health. 'He is not ill. He is indestructible. Get out of my room you snivelling little toads,' she says. And the nobles retreat.

GORBACHEV *about to ask a question, but she continues.*

The high officials are desperate. Potemkin's latest fit has lasted

for nearly a month. Documents requiring his signature are piling
up. The Empress will not listen. One day the officials were
gathered round the Chancellors' ante-room, when an
insignificant clerk named Shuvalkin entered. He saw their faces
and asked them what the problem was. They told him. He begged
them to give him the papers. At their wits' end they agreed, what
had they to lose? The clerk Shuvalkin took the documents and
started his long walk through the maze of corridors and galleries.

RAISA *performs a little mime of the walk.*

Finally he reaches the Chancellor's bedroom. Potemkin is sitting in
bed in a dirty nightshirt looking quite lost. Shuvalkin goes to the
writing desk, dips the quill in the ink and takes the papers to the
Chancellor and hands him the pen. 'Name?' asks Potemkin.
'Shuvalkin' replies Shuvalkin. The Chancellor takes the pen and
signs all the papers. The triumphant clerk takes the papers back
to the nobles. He hands them the papers. They grab them
eagerly. They stare in disbelief. Every document is
signed'SHUVALKIN'.

A pause.

GORBACHEV. Why tell me that, now?

RAISA. Because I'm scared. I don't want you ending up paralysed
like Potemkin.

GORBACHEV (*angrily*). I will never let the power and responsibility
of this office be stolen by the apparatus. Never Raya. Yesterday
our dear old comrade Alexander Dubček came to see me. We
talked about the Prague Spring and 'socialism with a human
face'. 'You know Mikhail Sergeyevich', he said, 'if perestroika and
glasnost had happened in 1968 we would not be in this situation
today'. I agreed. The third way, an open, humane socialist
democracy was destroyed by the same people who talk today
about perestroika destroying the nation. How dare they shout at
me! Dubček and I agreed, with sadness in our hearts, that it was
too late for a third way now, but it might revive in twenty years if
we succeed today. We hugged each other. It's a sad business,
making history under circumstances out of your control . . .

RAISA. Listen to me, Misha. Unlock everything! Say what you need
to say to the country. All of it. Now.

*He takes another towel and throws it around his shoulders toga-like. The
image of a Roman senator.*

GORBACHEV. Citizens. For five years I have thought that the party
as a whole could be won round to perestroika, yes, including
most of the apparatus. Well, I was wrong. It cannot be done. So –
let people form new political parties. The Communist Party can
only be rejuvenated through political competition. When we
started out I was sure that we could do it all, but history teaches
different lessons. The monopoly of the party is over. For ever.
Finished. It should never have been there in the first place.
Socialism without democracy is a nightmare, as you all know. The
post of General Secretary of the Communist Party is hereby
abolished. The nomenklatura and its privileges are abolished. All
special hospitals and clinics will be open to everyone.

RAISA. Not enough!

GORBACHEV. Comrades. We can no longer ignore the world
economy. We have been walking naked in the streets of Moscow
in mid-winter and pretending that it isn't cold. The transition to
a market economy will be painful, but necessary. Employment!
We can no longer evade the issue. It is cowardice to conceal
unemployment, that is to keep in the plants an excess number of
workers, male or female, some barely working, others not
working at all. There will be people out of work, perhaps many.
You will be angry but it has to be done, we cannot lead the
economy with an extinguished torch. There is no other way
because of where the dead have led us for the last fifty years.

RAISA, *another impatient gesture.*

Citizens. Democracy and a regulated market could give birth to
new possibilities. Yes, my friends, we will steal the Devil's spoon
and appropriate capitalism for social ends. We have accepted
German reunification. Perhaps we gave in too quickly. Perhaps I
should have appealed directly to the German people . . .

RAISA. Too late!

GORBACHEV. Still, it has come and Germany will be our natural
ally. Our children must be told the Great Patriotic War is over.
I'm sure this is right and we can have a nuclear-free Europe in
the next century. After a pact with Germany, a pact with Japan.
We will return the Kuriles to the Japanese in return for a trade
deal to computerise the Soviet Union. Then the Soviet Union
must become a true Commonwealth of Republics, which elects
members directly to the European Parliament. It is changes like
this that will make nationalism absurd. And, citizens, here I give

pride of place to Russian nationalism, the old dragon. Let us decapitate it forever! My future as a man and a politician is linked to the success of perestroika. If it fails, I fall. If it succeeds, everything is possible. The old party's over.

RAISA. They will kill you for this.

Scene Four

LIGACHEV, VICTOR, ZAIKOV and RIMMA *come forward, the corpse of* NIKOLAI CEAUŞESCU *dangling between them.* CEAUŞESCU *speaks as a ventriloquist's dummy, operated by* VICTOR.

CEAUŞESCU (*to* LIGACHEV). Who chickened out at the Twenty-eighth Party Congress then? Who wouldn't stand against Gorbachev? Who got thrown off the Politburo then?

LIGACHEV. Shut up!

CEAUŞESCU. What happened comrade Ligachev? Were you threatened? Did the KGB show you your file, with all your corruptions recorded? Ha! Did the Gorbachevites cut off your balls?

LIGACHEV (*hitting the dummy*). Shut up shut up shut up!

RIMMA. Comrade, please! Let us preserve our dignity! (*With great menace.*) And remind ourselves that we are still dangerous.

GENERAL GROMOV *appears. He is a fit fifty-years-old man, his back straight, his face handsome, his hair a fine silver and grey, his uniform immaculate. A silence. Then the* CEAUŞESCU *dummy, quietly, in awe.*

CEAUŞESCU. Look. A real man.

LIGACHEV. Comrade General Gromov! It is an honour to meet with the heroic veteran of the Afghanistan campaign.

RIMMA. Comrade General.

VICTOR. Comrade General.

ZAIKOV. We can only say to you, comrade, that we wish you had been given the opportunity to actually win the war.

GROMOV *gives a curt, disdainful nod of his head.* LIGACHEV *and his friends look at each other uneasily.*

VICTOR (*aside to* ZAIKOV). He doesn't say anything.

ZAIKOV (*to* VICTOR). Sh.

LIGACHEV. Comrade General, let us be frank. Our country is
falling to pieces. Law and order is breaking down. Our borders
are threatened by Muslim fanatics in the South, by neo-fascists,
raising Nationalist flags, at the heart of the Union, even in Russia
itself. The old reactionary forces rise from the grave, class
division, selfishness, even the disgrace of anti-semitism is rife
again. What citizen of what other country would not weep, if their
homeland were in the predicament of the Soviet Union today?
But along with other patriots, I find myself silenced. I cannot
believe that the Officer Corps will tolerate this state of affairs. (*To
his friends.*) Our generals are the most ideologically aware
generals in the world . . .

ZAIKOV. Brilliant men! Our generals are a match for most
members of the Central Committee.

LIGACHEV (*smiling*). Present company excepted of course.

Attempted laughter, they look at GROMOV, *who remains inscrutable.*

We would appreciate your understanding of the present
situation, comrade General.

ZAIKOV (*with a wheedling expression*). Yes General, what's going to
happen to your tank commanders in the old East Germany, your
infantry, your Military Intelligence staff . . . Is the Red Army going
to join Nato? Or are your comrade soldiers to be thrown into the
food queues, back home?

A silence. Then a single flick of GROMOV's *baton against his leg. An
uneasy pause. Then* RIMMA, *with a snarl.*

RIMMA. At least the food crisis keeps Gorbachev unpopular. As
long as the people are kept hungry, there's a chance they'll turn
round and eat him!

Sour laughter, but VICTOR *is po-faced.*

VICTOR. Politically speaking, of course.

CEAUŞESCU. Oh I don't know. We in Romania never flinched
from . . .

VICTOR *puts a hand over the dummy's mouth, which he, of course, is
operating. And, suddenly,* GROMOV *is speaking in a golden, manly
voice.*

GROMOV. Enough of jokes, enough of petty political malice.
Comrades, for the second time this century we're witnessing a
tragedy of centralism. In 1917, within the space of three hours,
the monarchy disintegrated. The Romanovs became part of
history. We recreated centralism through Stalinism. Terror. Fear.
In destroying one centralist idea and replacing it with another,
we lost tens of millions of our citizens. And today . . . (*He pauses.*)
Today our shaven heads are once again under the threat of an
axe. Perestroika is a form of self-destruction. The ideological
cement, the social vision of the future that united us, has
crumbled into dust. Hence the retreat to nationalisms. Our
galaxy has exploded. Black holes are everywhere. The attacks on
the central planning mechanism has made the economy
unmanageable. The Republics are taking over the industries
within their territory. Entire branches of the economy are
degraded. Our army, that guarantor of stability and sovereignty,
service in whose ranks united all our citizens, is being torn apart
by nationalism, desertion, breakdown in discipline. The Officer
Corps is totally paralysed. And the Party! The Party! This
organism which suffused our country's brawn with its nerve
tissues, reconciling a multi-national citizenry, this Party is being
destroyed. I will never forgive Mikhail Sergeyevich Gorbachev for
that.

LIGACHEV *and his friends suck in their breath.*

And now . . . the reunification of Germany, as Soviet foreign
policy! Once again the Germans are striding across the map of
Europe, with their angst, their arrogance, their sense of
superiority, their sentimental instability of character. What an
irony, eh? *We* defeated German fascism! Millions of our citizens
perished in that war. And now the same firms and companies
which constructed the crematoriums, and used the 'lower races'
as slave labour to increase their profit margins, these same firms
are now poised to enter Central and Eastern Europe. And the
Soviet Union? Never! We must fight back instead of lying
prostrate before the new German model tank – I mean the
Deutsche Mark. All the gains of 1917 have been squandered, I
agree. But the Bundesbank and the Frankfurt Stock Exchange
will not run this country. I will make a block with anybody,
including the devil, to save our people from the scourge of
German capitalism!

LIGACHEV *and the others applaud wildly and go to* GENERAL
GROMOV *embracing him, kissing him on the cheeks.* LIGACHEV

breaks away with a gesture to RIMMA.

LIGACHEV. I think so, don't you?

RIMMA. Yes comrade.

She hurries off in one direction. LIGACHEV *joins the group around* GROMOV *and leads them off in another.*

Scene Five

Moscow Airport. AIR TRAVELLERS *clamber up onto the table, with much luggage – huge dilapidated suitcases and bags, brown paper parcels, some with ancient airport trolleys piled high. Amongst the travellers there is a Buddhist monk, an Orthodox priest, a Georgian family, the mother wreathed in scarfs, one of the Leningrad rockers seen before, with guitars in cases. An air of confusion, anxiety and boredom.*
The airport announcements are loud and grating.

ANNOUNCER. Aeroflot flight 901 to Gottenburg is delayed.

A knot of travellers sags in despair. A Pepsi Cola VENDOR, *his arms full of bottles, moves amongst the crowd.*

VENDOR. Pepsi. Pepsi. Pepsi.

ANNOUNCER. Aeroflot flight 431 to Baghdad is cancelled.

BORIS *comes on. He is wearing a light brown corduroy suit. He carries suitcases. He puts them down and strides about excited.*

BORIS (*to the* VENDOR). Know anything about the flight to Florence?

VENDOR. Delayed an hour. You'll be OK.

BORIS. Thanks.

VENDOR. Watch yourself round here.

BORIS. What?

The VENDOR *nods at* BORIS's *suitcases, from which he has strayed.*

BORIS. Oh. Thanks.

The VENDOR *wanders away.* BORIS *sits down on his luggage, happily.*
ZOYA, LARISSA *and* GRISHA *come on, searching anxiously.*

ZOYA. There he is.

They confront BORIS, *who is alarmed to see them.*

BORIS. You won't stop me.

LARISSA. Florence? Is that where you're going?

BORIS. I'll teach there.

LARISSA. Teach what?

BORIS. Pasternak, Mandelstam, Akmatova . . .

LARISSA. Bastard.

BORIS. It's a University job!

LARISSA. Oh yes, you'll be fêted won't you? Will you go on Italian
television and talk of the latest horrors under perestroika?

BORIS. I . . . do know Italian TV people . . .

LARISSA. And what about us? Are you sneaking out of our
marriage, as well as away from your father and mother, not to
mention your country?

ZOYA. Larissa . . .

LARISSA. Your brother gave his life for this country. Along with the
other millions. Are you sneaking away from that too?

BORIS *explodes.*

BORIS. Oh the dead millions! The moral weight on the back of my
neck! I want to be rid of it. Well the millions who are still alive,
and young, want to get out. Have you seen the visa queue at the
Western embassies?

ZOYA *about to speak.*

LARISSA (*to* ZOYA). No, let me. (*To* BORIS, *quietly.*) Florence is just
a place, like any other. Where some are happy, some are in
misery.

BORIS. Yes, but not 'happy', not 'in misery' like here.

GRISHA. Boris.

He pauses.

Boris, how real is this job you've been offered?

BORIS (*heatedly*). What do you mean 'how real is it?' Professor
Bellario promised me I could lecture there.

GRISHA. When?

BORIS. When he was here in Moscow! He said I could lecture at the University.

GRISHA. Westerners do that. They turn up in Moscow, get excited in Red Square, make promises to the natives . . . Stupid, stupid boy, do you actually have a contract from this professor?

BORIS. He wrote to me!

GRISHA. Wrote a contract?

BORIS. And I'm in with the TV company. From Milan. I got right in with them, when they came here to do a programme on the Popular Front. They interviewed me, for godsake! Anytime, they said. Look! (*He takes out a pen.*) They gave me a pen. With the name of the TV station on it.

ZOYA (*to* GRISHA). He's gone mad . . .

LARISSA (*to* BORIS). I cannot believe it's you saying this . . . I cannot believe this naivety . . . You were a radical. You were one of the young lions, hard-headed, a critic of society, battling away. All those hours, talking into the night! Pamphlets, speeches on street corners . . . You were going to lead us all to a bright new future . . . now what are you doing, sitting in the airport in that silly suit?

BORIS *flicks his hand at her. Then clasps his hands. He is trembling.*

BORIS. Florence is a city of light. I want light. This country isn't a union of nations. It's a *prison* of nations. (*He looks at them, each in turn.*) How stupid you are. Look at yourself Larissa, with your face covered in Polish cosmetics. How many hours did you queue for that lipstick? And you, mother. You put on your scarf, as if you are a true peasant in the country air . . . but you're an office cleaner, in a polluted city . . . And you, Father . . for all your principles and agonising, what are you? An old policeman, trying to keep your spine straight and your medals shiny . . . (*He is near tears.*) You are all so . . . backward, so provincial . . .

ZOYA. How dare you . . .

LARISSA. Don't worry. He's scared.

BORIS. It . . . died in me.

ZOYA. Pfft! I never could understand intellectuals. How a son of mine ever became one I don't know. What do you mean? What 'died' in you?

A pause.

BORIS. The future. If Gorbachev hangs on, what will the country be like in ten years time? A second Brazil. Shanty towns. Gimcrack economics. Squalor. And if he goes, what? Back to the 1930s? Back to the nineteenth century? The four of us cutting frozen logs in Siberia? Or war at the turn of the century with Iran? Yeah why not, let the Muslims take over what's left of the Soviet Union. At least they believe in something. Gorbachev is finished, it's all going to pieces. It's terminal! Can't you see? The Kremlin will fall, you'll all go down in the mess. There's a whiff of the Black Hundreds in the air.

LARISSA. Sick, sick scared.

BORIS. How many do we know, from our old student circle, who've left already . . . ? Not just Jewish friends.

LARISSA. I . . .

BORIS. Count them!

LARISSA *is silent.*

I don't want to be left alone here.

GRISHA *kneels beside* BORIS.

GRISHA. Boris, listen. In the time of Brezhnev, in Pasternak's time, people like you were gold dust in the West. Glamorous heroes out of hell. And many who went were courageous, I'm not saying they weren't. But now? The United States has stopped Soviet Jewish immigration. You know what the West Germans call the flood of people from the East? 'White Turks'. We are not glamorous any more. To the West we are odd people in ugly suits, with ugly accents, turning up in London, Paris, Milan, Florence . . . thinking we'll be rich. And ending in a single room in a slum somewhere. You'll be nothing in the West.

BORIS. No. I'm young.

GRISHA. Don't you know what's happening? Home, the continent, even the planet . . . is becoming one . . . vast . . . room.

He smiles.

Mind you, what colour curtains and what kind of furniture

there'll be, is going to be a hell of an argument. We may get into building a whole new house . . . But we began it all, in the Soviet Union. We began a new age. Now we must try to live with it. Stay with us. If it goes wrong, die with us. We surely will.

A pause.

BORIS. Why should I believe you? You were a torturer.

BORIS *hangs his head. Then he stands stiffly. He speaks harshly.*

GRISHA. What Lenin said about infantile disorders? It's true. When the ultra Left go bourgeois, they really go . . . all the way.

He strides away and off the stage.

BORIS (*to* LARISSA). I want to live in a city of light. Don't you understand?

ZOYA *touches her arm.* LARISSA *about to speak.*

ZOYA. No, don't bother. He's not worth it. He's not my son, he's not a son of this country.

They walk away. BORIS *rubs his face and takes a deep breath. He looks at his watch. The three* GANGSTERS *come up behind him.*

1ST GANGSTER. To the gentleman's toilet, comrade.

BORIS. What?

The 2ND GANGSTER *appears to have a gun in his coat pocket. The* 3RD GANGSTER *strokes* BORIS's *shoulder and arm.*

3RD GANGSTER. You've got something we want.

2ND GANGSTER. Be sensible, man.

BORIS *is hastened away by the* GANGSTERS, *down a trap in the table. The queue of* AIR TRAVELLERS *stirs.*

AIR TRAVELLERS. My flight . . .

My flight . . .

My future . . .

My life . . .

They begin to sink beneath the stage.

– I want!

– I want!

– I want to own a plantation on the Israeli West Bank!

– I want to be a Munich businessman, fat with drinking beer!

– I want to do Jane Fonda workouts and marry the next
President!

– I want to be a professor at the Massachusetts Institute of
Technology! And work in the White House!

– I want to live in Los Angeles and have sex in the back of a
stretch limousine!

– I want!

– I want to buy a fashion house in Paris and eat in the restaurant
on the Eiffel Tower, every night!

– I want to own a fast food chain! Bigger than Kentucky Fried
Chicken!

– I want to see sunsets all around the world!

– I want six bank accounts in London, Paris, Madrid, Tokyo, New
York, Bangkok!

– I want to own three hotels in Miami and marry Madonna!

(*Unison*). – We want the West, we want to BE LIKE YOU . . .

They have nearly disappeared.

ANNOUNCER. Aeroflot flight 551 to Florence will leave from Gate
Number 12. All passengers for the Aeroflot flight to Florence,
please go to Gate Number 12.

The three GANGSTERS *hurry up from the trap, carrying* BORIS's
luggage. BORIS *follows them, bereft of his suit. He stands, lost, in his
boxer shorts, singlet, socks and shoes.*

ANNOUNCER. Would any remaining passengers for Aeroflot
flight 551 to Florence, please come to Gate Number 12. This is
the last call for the flight to Florence.

BORIS *pulls an air ticket and a wallet from his trunks.*

BORIS. Wait! Wait for me!

He starts to turn. Lights down.

Scene Five

GORBACHEV *runs onto the stage in a track suit, two* BODYGUARDS *running behind him.*

GORBACHEV *stops. He is out of breath, he rests. The* BODYGUARDS *rest.*

BORIS YELTSIN *comes on and clambers up onto the table. His flies are open and he is somewhat the worse for wear, having been up all night. The* BODYGUARDS *become alert.*

GORBACHEV (*to the* BODYGUARDS). No no, go on.

The BODYGUARDS *go off.*

YELTSIN. Ah! You look well, Mikhail Sergeyevich.

GORBACHEV. Good morning, Mr President! Been up all night, Boris?

YELTSIN, *the wave of a hand.*

YELTSIN. An affair of the heart.

A silence.

GORBACHEV. Have you ever breathed the night air over the abyss, Boris?

YELTSIN *stares at him.*

I have!

YELTSIN. I'm prepared to meet you half-way.

GORBACHEV. It doesn't mean anything, Boris. Five years of perestroika. You've enjoyed perpetual opposition. The prince, permanently waiting in the wings. Now you're on the stage, 'President of The Russian Federation'. But what are you going to do?

YELTSIN (*interrupting*). The people . . . the people are with . . .

GORBACHEV (*getting angry*). The people! We must once and for all rid ourselves of this Robespierrian delusion. We do not have the people in our pockets.

YELTSIN (*angry*). You don't. Have you ever joined a queue?

GORBACHEV. Queues, Boris? Queues? I know why you love queues. For the last five years you've been queuing for power. Politics, principles. What do they matter?

YELTSIN. You? You accuse me? Who was it who ganged up with the dead forces to remove me from the Politburo? Who manoeuvred against my supporters in Moscow? We started off on the same side, Mikhail Sergeyevich. You decided to break. Can't you feel what they're going to do? Your head is turning into chalk.

GORBACHEV. Dead forces, Boris? Who? We've removed the criminals. Grishin, Romanov . . . their cronies. Gone. How far do you want to go, Boris? Should we fire every corrupt station master on the Irtutsk line for selling cabbages on the sly? Should we sack the entire nation for corruption?

YELTSIN. Ligachev. Vorotnikov. Them.

GORBACHEV. Ah! A purge. (*He shakes his head.*) Fight them politically. In the very near future it is the people who will decide.

YELTSIN. You won't like what the people want, Misha. The Baltics want their independence. Do you like their flags? No.

GORBACHEV. The Ukrainians and Byelorussians want their independence. Do *you* like their flags? No.

YELTSIN. But Lithuania is a country that democratically has . . .

GORBACHEV. Lithuania is a what? I can't stand this ignorant romance. People are inventing nationalisms at the drop of a dollar. Imagined communities, nothing else. Look at the old maps. Eighteenth, nineteenth centuries. Where is it? The capital Vilnius was a town in Byelorussia. Before the war forty-five per cent of Vilnius spoke Yiddish. The rest Polish, German and Russian. Lithuanian was only spoken in the villages. Lenin gave them independence after the revolution. They set up a right-wing dictatorship under Antanos Smetano. Good, decent, patriotic anti-semites, Boris. Then Stalin did his shit with Hitler and got them back into the old Empire. They declared independence one day after Hitler invaded the Soviet Union. And today, my dear Boris, nobody in Vilnius speaks Yiddish any more. They didn't need Hitler to wipe out forty-six thousand Jews in three months. You're playing with fire.

YELTSIN (*quietly*). You cannot deny the people what they want.

GORBACHEV. If the people want to disembowel their neighbours, I will certainly deny them what they want.

YELTSIN. You've always misunderstood me. Deliberately! You are a cold fish. You do not understand the Russian soul.

GORBACHEV. I am sick and tired of fellow Russians talking about their souls. This Russian soul of ours Boris, what is it? Self pity, desperation and a bottle of vodka.

YELTSIN. When there is no food, vodka is a help. Why is there no food, Mikhail Sergeyevich, after five years of perestroika?

GORBACHEV. In those early days, Boris, you used to talk about social justice. Now you attack me for not introducing the free market tomorrow. You don't want any restraints at all. Or am I putting words in your mouth? Your mouth does open and shut a great deal on this matter.

YELTSIN. My position is clear, in my book . . .

GORBACHEV. Have you read your book?

A pause.

You write about endless visits to offices where you shout 'more food, more trains, more houses'. As if shouting is government. Is that how you would run the Union? (*Quietly.*) It's a dreadful book, Boris. You have an ego the size of a water melon.

YELTSIN (*angrily*). I wrote every word in my book! You always go on like this. As if you have no weaknesses.

GORBACHEV. My biggest weakness? A sense of superiority! But ever since I overcame this I am perfectly strong.

YELTSIN. Have you fixed the date for our first ever general election?

GORBACHEV. Have you decided on the name of your new party? Christian Democrats? Russian Orthodox Christian Democrats? Free Market Democrats? National Socialist Russian Memory Party?

YELTSIN (*smiling*). I love it when you're scared.

They both smile. YELTSIN *offers a hand.* GORBACHEV *offers his.*

We are on the same side, you know. It's me you need. Not the dead forces. Together we could transform this country. Russia alone could become a paradise. The California of Europe.

Their hands freeze and fall.

GORBACHEV. Look. There goes your mouth again, Boris. We must have no illusions about the free market. There will be social explosions if we put 15 million people out of work.

YELTSIN. People would accept temporary unemployment *if* they trust the leadership.

GORBACHEV (*a flash of anger*). Don't you have any sense of the dangers involved? What if the people don't accept it? Will you give our soldiers the order to open fire on millions of workers rioting for jobs?

ZOYA, LENA *and* KATYA *now move to the centre of the stage pushing the two men apart, and occupy that position.*

YELTSIN. Let's ask them.

ZOYA. My flat's been sold. I wake up one morning and find that Rimma Zhukova is my new landlady. Is this perestroika?

YELTSIN. Tell me Zoya – are you in favour of the free market?

ZOYA. Yes!

GORBACHEV. Are you in favour of everyone's right to work?

ALL THREE. Yes!

YELTSIN. Are you in favour of greater wealth in this country?

ZOYA. Yes!

GORBACHEV. And in favour of a new middle class, fifty times better off than you?

The THREE WOMEN *look at each other. Then angrily.*

ZOYA. No!

KATYA. No!

LENA. No!

The two men look at each other in silence.

GORBACHEV. We must keep control. Human beings must be at the centre of our society, we must have social justice.

YELTSIN. It's too late now. It's all or nothing.

GORBACHEV. We're working together now, aren't we?

YELTSIN. Are we?

YELTSIN, ZOYA, KATYA *and* LENA *go off.* ZOYA *has second thoughts and walks back to* GORBACHEV. *She holds his arm affectionately.*

ZOYA. Don't worry.

GORBACHEV. The fight isn't over yet.

GORBACHEV *turns.*

Three Russian Orthodox PRIESTS come on. They walk one behind each other. One carries a large, loose black bag. They stop. One nods to the others. They shift uneasily.

GORBACHEV. Good morning.

1ST PRIEST. My son.

GORBACHEV (*waving the BODYGUARDS on*). It's all right.

The BODYGUARDS hesitate, then go off.

Since . . . you would not expect me of all people, to believe in the afterlife . . . I try to do the best for what I have in this, eh?

The FIRST PRIEST smiles. The SECOND PRIEST takes a machine gun from beneath his robes and shoots GORBACHEV dead.
The loud sound of the beating wings of flocks of birds rising and of dogs barking in the distance.
Immediately GORBACHEV falls to the ground the THREE PRIESTS pull off their robes and false beards revealing themselves as the THREE GANGSTERS, one of them in BORIS's corduroy suit. They stuff the robes, beards and hats into the large bag. RIMMA ZHUKOVA runs on. They hand her the bag. She runs off one way, the GANGSTERS the other.
The BODYGUARDS run back on, agitated, guns in hand.
Slowly the entire cast climbs up onto the table from its upstage edge, looking at the dead man. The BODYGUARDS cover them with their weapons.
ZOYA steps forward.

FLYING TYPIST. At this stage, the two authors decided it could not end like this. It must end like this.

The cast disappear over the edge of the stage as GORBACHEV stands.
LENA comes forward with a coat, a hat, a newspaper and a stick. She gives them to GORBACHEV and goes off. GORBACHEV puts on the coat, hat and scarf and leans on the stick.
By some device the stage transforms itself . . . Chekhovian issues, silver birches, autumn leaves. RAISA comes up on a trap. A verandah table and two wicker chairs, she sitting in one. She is old.

RAISA. Some coffee, Misha?

He sits, tosses the newspaper on the table.

GORBACHEV. Thank you my darling.

She pours a cup and hands it to him.

RAISA. Any news?

GORBACHEV. Washington, Washington, Washington. (*He looks up.*) I wonder whether there are still leaves on those wonderful trees on the White House lawn.

RAISA. We will never see them again.

GORBACHEV. The news is bad. The Americans are in trouble. They're desperately short of wheat this year. Want our help.

RAISA. No! Their human rights record last year was atrocious!

GORBACHEV. Yes. But. (*He shrugs.*) The Soviet Union does not want the American people to be without bread.

He sips his coffee. Lights out.

Appendix

1. **Gold in Moscow**
   'As for the present, leaving history aside for the moment,
   I warn you I shall complain to the management.'

   Mikhail Bulgakov
   The Master and Margarita

For the past year Tariq Ali and I have been writing a 'perestroika'
play, entitled *Moscow Gold*, about the events in the Soviet Union from
1982 to now.

It is a huge undertaking, with 102 parts for 33 actors. It has called
for some 'perestroiking' of how plays are made, to encompass such a
great theme. The only model we had was the work of the great Soviet
theatrical genius Vsevelod Meyerhold. He attempted a theatre of
great breadth, trenchant but nimble-footed, which was not
documentary but 'living history', played out upon the stage at many
levels of meaning with many techniques. *Moscow Gold* does not
imitate the 'look' of his productions, but we have tried to learn from
his spirit. We combine satire and history, tragedy and farce, analysis
and song, dramatising the predicament of the citizens of the Soviet
Union both 'high' and 'low', Politburo members and people in the
food queues, as their country is traumatised by the Gorbachev
reforms and the multiple crises they have unleashed.

We have had some bizarre adventures with the play. At times
discussions with various theatre managements reached the hysterical
pitch of Mikhail Bulgakov's great backstage satire, *Black Snow*. A West
End commercial producer whom Ali and I approached refused even
to read the play and described us 'a menace to the British Theatre'.
The agent of a 'star' actor, asked to read the part of Gorbachev, was
spotted by one of our spies on the Metropolitan line shouting and
hitting the seat next to him with the script. We take these as
encouraging signs that we are on the right track. *Moscow Gold* will
open in a production by the RSC, to their credit, on the main stage of
the Barbican Theatre on September 20th.

'To speak of these things is like kerosene in the mouth.'
(**A young Muscovite** to **H.B.**)

Tariq Ali has visited the Soviet Union a number of times. I had
never been, so, last summer, before we began writing, I went to
Moscow and Kiev for two weeks alone, setting myself the rule that I

would speak to no other Westerners, a wise decision: the Americans were a pain in the arse when you came in their orbit, finding Red Square 'so *small*', or loudly asking in a state restaurant whether the food before them was meat or fish, a spurious question since clearly no one, not even the cooks, could answer it.

It took some days and many conversations until the force of the obvious truth about Soviet citizens hit me, with anything like the realisation of what it meant. I was amongst Sunday afternoon crowds strolling along Arbat Street, with its restored nineteenth-century façades. There was a heatwave. The sun blasted down through the pollution, the queues at the occasional Pepsi-Cola stands were long and patient. Poets took turns to recite from heart – some received rapturous applause, others none. And the obvious came to me – everyone in sight in the street was in some way *a survivor*, and the child of survivors.

In England it is a casual thing to ask a chance acquaintance 'Are your mother and father still alive, what do they do?' To ask that in Moscow is a serious and sorrowful matter. The stories of tragedy and suffering pour out. This woman in her late fifties saw her parents murdered by German soldiers, and with her younger sister walked the roads for a month, before being taken in and brought up by a family of peasants. This man was in the camps for ten years and says, 'I lost a lung', then shrugs, 'one lung, one life left'.

And for anyone who came to maturity before 1985, who is 25 or older, there are the meaner, soul destroying experiences of survival under Brezhnev, the 'stagnation era', of which I repeatedly heard the phrase 'you couldn't breathe'. Everyone had to live in the halitosis of the terminally decaying bureaucracy – which everyone, but for a handful of relatively unimportant dissidents, serviced, half-awake in a kind of lethargic complicity. The Russian joke about the worthlessness of the rouble, 'I'll pretend to work, you pretend to pay me', sums up the economic disaster this complicity has caused. A man about my age, 47, said, with black Muscovite irony, 'At least under Stalin you had the choice of dying, screaming; under Brezhnev even that was denied to you'.

We should not be cheaply moralistic about 'corruption', the practical way to survive in such a world. We should remind ourselves how British teachers, doctors and lower-ranking civil servants feel powerless against the waves of Thatcherism's mad, bureaucratic edicts ('Health is a commodity', 'Learning to read is a marketplace' etc. etc.). Good people find their imagination stunted and their morale sapped, and roll over, 'going along with it all' – a very 'Brezhnev era' sentiment I hear in England all the time.

'They who fall behind are finished.'

Mikhail Gorbachev to **Erich Honecker**,
while kissing him in East Berlin, 7th October 1989

In *Moscow Gold* we have tried to grasp the Byzantine, multi-
dimensional 'unreal-reality' of the society in which Gorbachev and
the reformers in the Communist Party of the Soviet Union exploded
the twin programmes of glasnost and perestroika in the April of
1985.

We are not dewy-eyed about the conditions in the Soviet Union as
it lurches between disintegration and transformation. We give full
voice to the present chaos and bitterness. It is appalling to witness
the food crisis in Moscow's supermarkets, and terrible to sense the
humiliation and sorrow of a silent crowd in the Gum footwear
department, staring at the ranks of unwearable shoes, buying
nothing. ('Why is everyone here?' I asked. It turned out there was a
rumour that there were some good sandals from Czechoslovakia on
their way.) There were times in Moscow, and certainly in Kiev talking
to a leader of the National Front, a mad child of the Brezhnev era on
the rebound with his mind blasted by dangerous ideas, when it was
hard to contain a rage against what has been done in the Soviet
Union to the humanist aspirations of the founders of socialism.

But we do give notice that we are, perhaps unfashionably,
optimistic. Thomas Pynchon, in his brilliant new novel *Vineland*,
writes hilariously of the need for 'tube detoxification', that is drying
out from the effect of too much television. *Moscow Gold*'s authors
have constantly needed detoxification from television news and
punditry about the Soviet Union over the last year. For despite
almost weekly alarms of 'ultimate showdowns' and 'final collapse' in
the Western media, the nation of survivors endures and persists
upon its unique course of history. The 1917 revolution was unique;
the petrified forest of the Brezhnev era unique, and now there is the
unprecedented attempt of a decayed, authoritarian system to reform
itself, to turn itself inside out from within. Western socialists have for
years felt the dead hand of the disaster of Stalin and Brezhnev upon
their hopes. But now socialism is released. The end of the Cold War
can cut either way, and the triumphalism of the right may be
short-lived. In ten years' time, if the pessimists are right, the Soviet
Union will be 'Brazilified', a country rich in resources but sunk in
social misery. If the optimists, amongst whom Tariq Ali and I count
ourselves, are right, in ten years' time the Soviet Union will be a
commonwealth of nations with a new, democratic socialism up and
running, regulated market and all, and the 'Internationale' will once

again mean something.

One more thing about the theatre . . . *Moscow Gold* is nothing if not ambitious. There is a lot of talk about the end of the possibility of a vibrant political drama on publicly owned (that is 'subsidised') stages in Britain, killed off by hostile Thatcherite placemen in the Arts Council and the blandishments of commercial sponsors, for whom *Hamlet* is not a play but a 'logo opportunity'. Well! If a living theatre, 'alive to what it's like to be alive now', is to be killed off on the British stage, it is our intention, with plays like *Moscow Gold*, to make the funeral a very noisy and memorable party. And if the *Moscow Gold* team does its job well, the funeral may be so enjoyable it will not be we who end up in the grave.

Howard Brenton

(First published in *Marxism Today*)

2. How Can We do It, Vsevolod?

On the 14th of March, 1936, fighting for his theatre and for his life, the revolutionary Russian theatre director Vsevolod Meyerhold made a ferociously uncompromising and complex speech at the Soviet Writers' Union attacking 'socialist realism'.

He was defending himself against the Stalinist crime of 'formalism'. His argument was an immemorial one that would have been recognised by Euripides: 'the artist becomes a true master by endless observation, reflection and study, by consolidating form and content'. He attacked what he called 'Meyerholditis', the use of what *looked* like the political theatre he had invented but which was drained of any sense of what people were really thinking and doing, of any real dialectic – bravely he was trying to turn the tables on his tormentors, accusing the hacks of a dead 'formalism'. He spoke for a protean theatre that is experimental, in which form is never fixed but capable of infinite invention to serve its content, in a way a theatre without an aesthetic at all – but which is on the side of the ruled and not the rulers, and plugged directly into reality. He compounded the offence by going on to defend Shostakovitch's banned opera, *The Lady Macbeth of the Mtsensk District.*

The speech cost him both his theatre and his life. Because of 'glasnost' we now know how he died; he was murdered by the NKVD in the Lubianka prison on February 2nd 1940, after his fingers had been broken one by one and urine had been poured over his head.

When I was in Moscow last summer I visited the one shrine there is to Meyerhold's mighty work. In a little theatre museum in a quiet, tree-lined street, I was ushered into a room crammed with just about every memento of a great career that the secret police did not smash. I was the only visitor. As a guide droned on I stopped listening, because the dilapidated set models for shows that once entertained thousands, the yellowed posters, the typescripts of texts scribbled with pencilled notes, began to pulsate with life.

Meyerhold's output was of great variety. He could bash out a thumping, militant, pro-revolutionary extravaganza, then turn to a subtle reworking of a Russian classic, with the text untouched. He premiered new plays, most famously by Nikolai Erdman and Vladimir Mayakovsky, satires against Moscow gangsters and party time-servers. He premiered, and revived in the teeth of state disapproval, Mikhail Bulgakov's *The White Guard*, a great and tragic play that was considered dangerous because it dramatised the doomed humanity of a group of pro-Tsarist officers in the Civil War.

He concocted spectacles addressing issues of the day. The four strands of work ran side by side – outright political extravaganzas, renewal of the classics, new plays by living playwrights, and 'issue plays'. And all the work was shot through with a kind of madness: he had a barmy theory of acting, 'biomechanics', which was a reaction to the Stanislavsky school, and he was endlessly drawing up plans for a huge, fantastical and probably unworkable auditorium. His wonderfully attractive, mercurial craziness came from a sense of showmanship, of flair and a love of the new.

Like most Russian theatre directors, the man was also a fearsome martinet, I know. But he sensed that to do something really profound in the theatre, you should not take the theatre itself too seriously. He was a relentless perfectionist, whose work was informed by a contempt for orthodoxies, including his own, and always on the side of the ruled, not the rulers. Staring at the detritus of his career in that dusty Moscow museum, I began to see how a political theatre can be a living drama about changing our lives – not a sermon, but an event.

I write about Meyerhold because it's important to remind ourselves that the left too has its twentieth-century martyrs. It is insulting to the memory of a great artist to suggest that 'the theatre should not engage in political themes'. That is exactly what Meyerhold did, trenchantly, and with such success that the predecessors of those now called 'conservatives' in the Soviet Union had him murdered.

Tony Harrison, who translated Aeschylus' *Oresteia* for the National Theatre, told me that the *The Eumenides*, with its famous Aeschylean moral, 'the doer shall suffer', was probably very near the bone for its first audiences. There was violence in Athens between immigrants and the longer established communities, exasperated by a religious clash. The play dramatises a settlement. We assume the meaning of the play is so lofty as to be almost beyond human comprehension – actually it was written straight out of contemporary troubles, for life and about life, tackling a hot contemporary subject (would Bradford's Aeschylus please come to the stage).

I remember watching the National's production with mounting panic. Aeschylus is credited with inventing 'the play' as we know it. He seemed, what's more, to have made up every playwright's trick in the book in one go – think of a dramatic device, oh . . . realism, humour mixed with tragedy, chorus, disguise, revelation, 'high and low' on the stage, the powerful off-stage character . . . and it's there embedded in *The Oresteia*. The theatre is a profoundly archaic art. Meyerhold demonstrated that, paradoxically, that's why it can be such a vibrant modern form: since everything has been done before, you can find a way of putting *anything* on a stage.

But what you cannot do is write generally, or, sin of sins, to write 'for posterity' – our contemporary theatre is littered with the corpses of plays that took themselves too lightly or far too seriously, but above all too vaguely. As Meyerhold proved, the theatre is capable of endless renewal, if it rolls up its sleeves and gets stuck into what really matters in its day, what is really going on and fights a real fight. There is an infinite variety of ways of making theatre, but only one theme which, inevitably, Aeschylus was onto – it's simply 'how can we live justly?' Recall a great play or a great comic's act that you have enjoyed, *The Three Sisters* or Jacques Tati, and at root that will be the brazenly political theme.

Howard Brenton
(First published in *The Independent*)

3. Excerpts from a Diary

1985

London – Moscow, 24 April

Got the 11 a.m. flight to Moscow from Heathrow. Departure lounge surrounded by a set of vultures. Tabloid photographers. A Soviet diplomat has been expelled. From inside the plane I see the expelled diplomat arriving together with his over-dressed wife. They wave to the vultures and board the flight. I make notes for my speech at a United Nations University Conference on 'Security and Peace in Asia' in Tashkent, I am determined to talk about Afghanistan. The fact that the conference is sponsored by the UNU makes it easier, but . . .

At Moscow airport the customs search is thorough. A collection I've edited for Penguin Books, *The Stalinist Legacy*, is vetted by three men. They notice I have a dozen copies. One of them looks nervous. They look at the contents list: Trotsky, Rakovsky, Deutscher, Mandel, Anderson, Khrushchev, Dubček, etc. Then I point to my name on the cover. 'Ah! It's by you.' I smile. 'You need it for the conference.' I nod. The books are let through. I'm met and transported to the Hotel of the Academy of Sciences.

Moscow, 25 April

A tour of Moscow for all the delegates going to Tashkent. Why do they bother to have guides at all, when a tape-recorder will do? It's a wasted morning since I've seen the sights before.

At one-thirty, Dmitri, a 23-year-old student picks me up to take me to the flat of a senior lecturer at the oriental institute. Dmitri, an expert on Pakistan, insists on practising his Urdu on me! Over lunch, Natalia, an old friend of the parents, discusses the whole world, but not the Soviet Union. Konstantin Chernenko, king of the gerontocracy, has just died. I am curious about his successor, but neither of them has anything to say. Later, talking to Dmitri as he takes me round the bookshops – where there is nothing on offer – I find out that he is really far more interested in the Beatles than Pakistan. This is a relief. When he discovers that I actually knew John Lennon, my stock rises phenomenally.

Dev Murarka, an Indian friend who has been in Moscow for centuries, collects me for dinner. An Azerbaijani restaurant. Drunken officials, loud music, vulgar dancing and mediocre food. Despite the ambience Dev talks endlessly about conditions in the

Soviet Union. Awful. A secret report has confirmed that alcoholism results in widespread sterility, with twenty-five per cent of Russian babies being born with deformations. Dev insists that changes are on the way. 'The new man is an instinctive reformer'. Like Khrushchev? I'm not sure I believe him.

Moscow – Tashkent, 26 April

To Moscow's internal airport for a four-hour flight to Tashkent in Soviet Central Asian capital of Uzbekistan. There are some like-minded souls on the plane. All delegates. On arrival we are driven with a motorcycle police escort to a Party guest house 16 kilometres out of the city. The dinner is terrible. After dinner I convene a caucus of like-minded souls. The delegates from New Zealand, Malaysia, Fiji and Australia assemble to discuss the Congress. I warn them that I am not going to keep silent on Afghanistan. There is some nervousness.

The conference organiser, Mushakoji, is a delightful man with strong Samurai features. Our two interpreters, Natasha and Oxanne, are funny, cynical and relaxed. These are good signs. The Soviet delegation is hierarchically seated at the dinner table, but there are lots of younger faces – people in their fifties, forties and even thirties.

Tashkent, 27 April

Woke up at five a.m. and went with Kevin (New Zealand delegate) for an hour-long jog through the Uzbek countryside and villages. The security guards at the Party guest house astonished at our nerve. The guest house itself, I'm sure, serves as a trysting place for tired bureaucrats. It has that air about it. Gave my speech at the seminar. A friendly debate with the Soviet delegates on Afghanistan. More than friendly. Amazing. The line seems to be that they want to pull out, but the Americans and Pakistani military intelligence don't want peace. I was attacked by a CIA man masquerading as a Thai delegate, but the rest of the debate was constructive. In the lunch break a number of Soviet delegates came and hugged me. One of them said: 'We never thought we would hear such a speech in our country in our lifetime.' A very frank exchange of views followed. Something is changing. That much is obvious. Another Soviet delegate came up and told me: 'Your position on Afghanistan seems to be the same as Gorbachev's.' Our interpreters, too, are excited. So. It moves!

Went out in the evening to see Tashkent. It is a modern, if not a

modernist city. Earthquakes have destroyed a great deal of history.
Lots of ugly buildings. Natasha jokes: 'We call this the Chernenko
style in architecture. Dead!' We end for dinner at the Intourist
Hotel in the city. Food: awful! Uzbek dance style: nice. Music:
proto-rock. On the fringes of the hotel there are odd scenes taking
place. A man is beating his wife as if it were an everyday occurrence.
A black student is pleading, unsuccessfully, to be allowed to enter
the hotel. The faces of Uzbek officialdom: over-fed corruption.
Complacent. Cynical. Brutal. One of them, who also hangs out in
the Party guest house, approaches and offers me a prostitute for the
evening. One Asian to another! I decline politely. The Uzbek
leader, Old Corruption itself, Rashidov, has died suddenly. 'A
heart-attack,' someone mutters. 'Are you sure it wasn't suicide?' I
ask. There is a tense silence.Our party breaks up. On the coach
back to the guest house, Natasha whispers in my ear: 'How did you
know? It's meant to be a secret!' She doesn't believe me that I just
guessed.

Tashkent, 29 April

Last day of conference, mostly taken over by receptions. A deadly
event at Friendship House where the main speaker pays tributes to
Harold Wilson as an architect of USSR-Great Britain Friendship!
What! In the evening a farewell banquet with excellent local food. I
am seated next to Dr Nodari Simonia, a Soviet delegate. 'Are you in
the mood for drinking vodka or talking?' It is an interesting
counterposition. I opt for talking. N. tells me about Gorbachev.
They are expecting great things from him. 'For thirty years we have
been suffocated. When Gorbachev became First Secretary we
heaved a collective sigh of relief. There will be big changes.' I probe
further, but N. is totally confident. 'We know him. We've talked to
him. He's interested in new ideas, new thinking.' N. is from
Georgia. He has an interesting story about Stalin. 'You know my
grandfather used to tell us a very interesting tale. He was an old
Bolshevik. Joined the party several years before 1917. He was a
printer in Tiflis (Tblisi). He said he never trusted Stalin. When he
came to collect clandestine leaflets from my grandfather's
underground workshop he never looked my grandfather in the eye.
Anyway, come the revolution and everyone was celebrating in our
family circle. Then twenty years later, Stalin asked all Georgian old
Bolsheviks to declare themselves and be awarded special medals or
whatever. They all came to my grandfather. He warned them. "Best
to let him think we're dead", he told his old comrades. They
laughed at him. Every single one of them was killed. My grand-

father, who did not declare himself, lived to over a hundred years!'

On Afghanistan N. says that he agrees with me completely. They should never have gone in. He wrote a special paper for the Politburo before they went in, advising against the move. Andropov was sympathetic, but Brezhnev wanted to do something. 'Then they got someone to denounce my paper'. 'Who?' 'One of their favourite "prostitutes". I'm sure you can guess.' I do. This is the first real conversation I have had with a Soviet communist. No banalities. No frills. To the point.

Samarkand, 30 April

We are off to the magical city. I say my farewells to the leader of the Soviet delegation, Yevgeni Primakov [now an alternate member of the Politburo – T.A.], who invites me to come again, spend more time and talk. 'I'm not being polite. This is a serious invitation.' Then we fly to Samarkand. The mosques, beautifully preserved, are a sensational example of Islamic architecture. The open market here is a joy. Unlimited supplies of fruit, food, nuts, dried fruits, silks, satins – an explosion of colour. A four-hour lunch at a model collective farm. A gross-out in every way. Get the guests to over-drink and over-eat. Follow this by a dance performance. Show them a few well-fed animals and happy collective farm workers; put on smiles as they depart and get paid for a day's work. This Stalinist model is so depressingly familiar. I have seen it in North Korea and China already, but the master-pattern was woven here, in the USSR. Ugh!

Tashkent, 1 May

The city is bedecked with red flags. We're taken to the reviewing stand as 'honoured guests'. A march-past lasting two hours. Boring and ritualistic. One point of interest. Apart from the portraits of the Politburo and Marx, Engels and Lenin, there is a young-looking Sergei Kirov as well! The man whose assassination (by Stalin) was the pretext for the first massive purge of old Bolsheviks.

In the evening our interpreter Natasha invites us for a meal. 'My Igor is getting jealous. He'd better meet all of you.' We buy the raw materials from the open air market and repair to her apartment, where, to Igor's amazement, I cook the meal. Then we talk till the early hours. Trotsky, Bukharin, the wiping out of the Old Guard. Khrushchev's attempt to de-Stalinise. The dinner becomes an animated discussion on history.

Natasha is amazed to hear us defending Khrushchev. She has

accepted the Brezhnev line on him, and we argue. Igor grins. It
emerges they have been having this argument for years, and he is
delighted with our support. She asks how we know so much about
Soviet history. I tell her, 'It's our history as well'. Now Natasha talks
openly of the situation in Uzbekistan. The corruption, Rashidov's
suicide, etc. But all Rashidov's men are still in place. Suddenly it
seems clear. In this part of the world the old pre-capitalist structures
of society merged happily with the command-system of Stalinism.
The language was different, but the practice was the same. Can
nothing change the politics of the Oriental bazaar?

Stories. Rashidov feeling like a fuck. A Russian woman staying at
the Party guest house. He sends for her. She is drunk and insists
on riding to his place on the bonnet of the car, breasts bare and her
hair flying. In this fashion she travels twenty kilometres. This is not
all. In the back seat of the car some poultry is being carried for
comrade Rashidov. In the centre of Tashkent late one night a
bystander sees the naked woman. Then he sees a cock flying out of
the back window and the woman laughing. Is this real or a Buñuel
movie. Real!

Stories. A reception in honour of Brezhnev. One of Rashidov's
acolytes presents Rashidov with a gold statuette of himself. The
local leader smiles . Brezhnev feels the statuette. 'Can we be so bold
as to commission a large one like this of you comrade?' Rashidov
asks Brezhnev with fake humility. Brezhnev nods. The next day he is
given a gold statue. Corruption? No. Local traditions of hospitality.

Moscow, 12 May

Back in Moscow. I meet an old friend. Tell him what N. has said
about expectations of Gorbachev. He laughs cynically. He has seen
it all before. 'Look my friend. There's always hope when a new Tsar
is crowned.'

1988

Moscow, 20 April

Invited to Soviet Union as a guest of the Writers' Union. Met at
Moscow by Mariam (Mira) Salganik from the Union and an
interpreter. Mira speaks excellent English. Am plonked in the hotel
Rossiya. Brezhnevite architecture at its worst, and this hotel must be
the largest brothel in the world. An elaborate free-market of pimps
and prostitutes is in operation. No doubt the state gets a cut!

Dinner at the Writers' Union club. The dining room used to be the ballroom in the mansion of a former Countess. Mira says she returned last year, saw the place and muttered; 'Always knew the Bolsheviks would not be able to maintain this place . . . ' Could this be the same Writers' Union described by Bulgakov in *The Master and Margarita?* No, alas, that was a different building. And yet the atmosphere is not so different. The Union, in reality, acts as the ideological police of Brezhnevism. Mira is very exceptional. The place is packed with careerists high on alcohol and their own mediocrity. The atmosphere is totally transformed. Everyone is talking politics. Everyone has a view. Mira is totally immersed in the factional struggle inside the Party. She is a hard-line Gorbachevite and confirms that the party is bitterly divided. And Yeltsin? 'Very popular, but too much of a populist and not very bright!'

Moscow, 21 April

Visited the offices of *Ogonyok*, which is the most innovative of the glasnost magazines. Korotich, the editor, was abroad as usual, but his deputy talked for a few hours. His hostility to Yeltsin smacked of careerism to me. When I pushed him he said: 'Yeltsin is like Stalin!' I exploded. He explained, 'He's a workaholic. Works till late and expects his employees to stay in the office too.' I said that the solution for them was clear. They should threaten strike action! There is still too much of 'loyalty' to the new line. It's still difficult to work out what some people really think!

At 4 p.m. went to Boris Kagarlitsky's flat. In his early thirties, B. has been formed by Western Marxism and reading the *New Left Review*. Fascinated by the sixties in Western Europe. The best-read person in Moscow and incredibly talented, with more than a whiff of ultra-leftism. He is a leading light in the Moscow Federation of Socialist Clubs. After tea and cake he drags me willingly to a meeting of the F-Soc Executive, where I sit through a five-hour meeting. There is a very strong feeling of *déjà-vu* here. It could have been the meeting of one of the far-left groups in Western Europe in the sixties or seventies. The comrades in Omsk are complaining that the paper is badly printed. The comrades in Leningrad ask why all the key documents are written in Moscow. Socialists in the Urals want some equipment to be sent to them so that they can produce their own material. Met among others Victor Gershfeld, a former Colonel in the Red Army, who defended Moscow against the Nazis when he was fourteen. He is a member of the Party and active in the Socialist Clubs. A fascinating man. He agreed to be interviewed at length and we fix a date. (See pp.102-110.)

Moscow, 22 April

Interview Otto Latsis, a slightly dour Latvian who is the Deputy
Editor of the party's theoretical journal, *Kommunist*. He is guarded.
Still defends the notion of a one-party state but admits under
questioning that this notion does not flow from socialist theory.
Later I walk through the Arbat. Good second-hand bookshops.
Bought a special 1921 edition of a magazine devoted to the work of
Dostoevsky. No first editions of Lenin or Bukharin available yet. All
Lenin's first editions were banned, and only doctored versions were
available for decades. But the woman knows of private libraries
where they exist and promises that on my next trip she'll have
them. And Trotsky? 'Perhaps in a few years, but very few people hid
those. So it will be more difficult.'

In the evening to the Komsomol Theatre to see Shatrov's
Dictatorship of Conscience, a glasnost play. Mixture of Brechtian
agitprop and Shatrov's version of history. Skeleton of play is a mock
trial of Lenin. Witnesses for the prosecution include Churchill,
Hemingway and a French Stalinist. Very mixed audience: the
atmosphere is electric with applause and cheers for the attacks on
Stalinism and Brezhnevism. Red Army officers and soldiers in
audience are interviewed impromptu by the actor playing Engels . . .

Moscow, 23 April

Exhausting day. I try and jog alongside the Volga every morning to
survive the day, but it didn't work today. Met the professors of
journalism at Moscow University. They appear shell-shocked by
glasnost. Ghosts from the Brezhnev era. For years they've been
teaching rubbish. They defend the party's monopoly of
information. I ask: 'Are you excited by the new trend of investigative
journalism?' There is no answer. I realise that they find my question
shocking. What will happen to people like them?

At dinner Mira tells me that Gorbachev's real speech last
November for the Anniversary of the Revolution was not delivered.
The Politburo insisted on changes, and he was forced to back down.
The speech he did make was a weak and watery reflection of the
original. While we were eating, a musicologist acquaintance of M.'s
came to our table. He was in a state of advanced inebriety. He saw
me and asked my country of origin. I told him. 'Pakistan! You know
my nephew was captured by the Afghan mujahideen. They
castrated him. Stuffed his penis in his mouth, skinned him alive and
sent his body back. What do you think of that?' I expressed shock,
horror. 'So you don't defend them?' No. He was puzzled. He

wanted the Soviet troops out. We agreed. My attack on the practices of the Afghan rebels bothered him. We discussed nationalism. I told him I was a rootless cosmopolitan. Did not feel loyal to any state. 'Ah!' he said. 'A Trotskyite!' What an insightful drunk!

Moscow, 28 April

Went to visit Victor Gershfeld. His bookshelves lined with German editions of Goethe and Marx. Victor is a German-Russian, immensely cultured and refers affectionately to Gorbachev as 'Mishenka'. We talk on tape for several hours about everything . . .

Moscow, 11 October

Back in Moscow for a conference on the cinema. Ken McMullen introduces his film *Zina* on Trotsky's daughter. It is well received. Afterwards, talking to S., a post-graduate student heavily into post-modernism, I am slightly surprised to hear him defending Dostoevsky's anti-semitism. The films we have seen have had a mystical, religious streak running through them. I complain to S., but he defends the Church. 'Our intelligentsia has always been influenced by Christianity.' I remind him of 1917. 'Oh that was the Jews.' So much for the Revolution. A canvas painted by the wicked Jews! Later that day I mentioned this to Boris K., and he laughed. He regards this sort of anti-semitism as ugly, but harmless.

Moscow, 13 October

The Bulgarian delegates to the conference express a yearning for perestroika in their country. I promise them that it will come! Dinner at 'Pirosmani', an excellent co-operative restaurant with Jonathan and Ruth Steele and Fred Jameson. Jonathan has brought his own wine along which is a relief. J. is convinced that the Soviet example is going to spread to Eastern Europe. It's only a matter of time. We agree. He is also pretty confident that it will be impossible for the conservatives to dump Gorbachev. Numerous Moscow intellectuals say the same thing. 'If we fail it will be a social and political Chernobyl' is a common phrase.

Moscow, 14 October

Dined with V.M., a brilliant academic who is in the party and very active in the struggle. He thinks that the aim of the conservatives is to 'integrate Gorbachev' into the apparatus so totally that he is suffocated by the hug and becomes one of them. V. thinks this is a danger. He feels that unless the system is opened up quickly the party reformers could lose all credibility. The apparatus has to be dismantled. He is passionate on this question.

Tariq Ali

4.   **From the Dictatorship of Weakness to a Democracy of Strength**
An Interview by Tariq Ali with Victor Alexandrovich Gershfeld,
Moscow, 1988

Ali: Could you tell me something about your early life. What sort of
family did you come from? How did you view the Revolution?

Gershfeld: I was born in Moscow. My grandparents were doctors.
My grandfather also was in the army – he was an officer in 1905 and
1914, it was an old family tradition. If you go to Khiva, for example,
there at the local history museum you can see a picture with the
following inscription: 'The generals Gershfeld and Garkhin are
giving the command to attack.' Both my grandfather and
grandmother were communists. My grandfather joined the party in
the first days, and my father joined the Bolsheviks in 1918. At the
time he studied at Moscow University, and it is from there that he
joined the Red Guards first and then went into the Red Army and
fought in the Civil War. Later on he directly reported to Lenin on
the state of affairs at the front. In *Izvestia* a map used to be
published with the latest developments at the front, signed by my
father. Until 1931 he held high posts, being a general in the army.
Then he started having some difficulties.

Ali: Do you remember your father ever talking about Trotsky or
Tukhachevsky?

Gershfeld: Of course the families of the old Bolsheviks knew each
other very well, and they used to meet quite often. My father met
Trotsky very often in the war, and once they had a clash. In the early
twenties my father was in charge of some troops in the Ural steppes,
in 1920 that was. A revolt was shaping up, and – just in case – my
father put the Tsarist officers under house arrest because the
Kulaks without military commanders were not a real force. Things
were very soon sorted out, but afterwards he was summoned by
Trotsky, removed from his command post and sent to the Military
Academy to study.

   Of course, that was just the one case, but what I want to say in
general here is that there is one fact which many of Trotsky's
biographers overlook. They call him a leftist, being of very radical
left views, but what they forget is that it was he who involved Tsarist
officers and had some patronage over them. The famous General
Rasilov rallied officers around himself in the Red Army on the eve
of the attack on Poland. Along with other things, it just proved that
Trotsky was a very sober-minded intellectual. His leftist views were
not manifested in his practical deeds.

After the war my father had some differences with Trotsky on the principles of building the Red Army, because Trotsky was for a sort of police system, a militia system on the Swedish pattern. My father believed that, from the point of view of the history of this country and the future of the army and state, we needed a permanent standing army, and I think my father was right. But once again this shows that Trotsky was not the type that drove the people by force into the army or into the so-called labour armies; on the contrary, he had quite liberal views even as far as the army was concerned. And this is what should be underlined and emphasised nowadays.

My father was younger than Tukhachevsky, and he was his junior in every respect, in age as well as in rank. He had great respect for Tukhachevsky, and I must say that at that time the circle of people who made up that political and economic society was quite narrow, quite small, so they all lived, worked and fought together. Tukhachevsky was a brilliant commander, and he and his group were the thinkers and pioneers of military art: not only in this country, but up to the Second World War, they were the most brilliant in the whole world. The military exercises, the war games in the mid-thirties, showed that the Red Army, except for its lack of technology, was at the time the best in terms of practical training, because it had had the unique experience of military manoeuvring in the Civil War, while the First World War had been mainly trenches. In this respect, the Civil War was the forerunner of World War Two.

Ali: Could we return to your father?

Gershfeld: Having quarrelled with Rasilov and those who determined the political making of the army he took up a diplomatic post. He became First Secretary of the Soviet Embassy in Germany. At that time his brother Eugene was First Secretary of the Soviet Embassy in France. He remained in this diplomatic work until 1937 and was quite familiar with Litvinov at that time. In the thirties he used to go personally to Stalin from Germany and then the usual happened: his brother was arrested and my father had to part with his party card for not being able to expose the enemies of the people. Stalin demanded in 1938/39 that he renounce his brother. I must say that my father got off quite lightly because he remained out of a job for a number of years and then started working for the Academy of Sciences.

Ali: But your uncle was killed?

Gershfeld: He was killed in 1941 in the panic when the troops were retreating from Moscow, but without any trial. The Germans were in the suburbs. My father and I joined the People's Militia, the volunteers recruited to defend Moscow. I was about sixteen. After that battle of Moscow, being a youngster still, I was sent back home.

Ali: But did you actually participate in the defence?

Gershfeld: I did, and I returned to the army in 1944 in the rank of sergeant. Towards the end of the war I was sent to military school, the one named after the Supreme Soviet, and afterwards up to 1959 served in the army. I left the army during Khrushchev's campaign to reduce the size of the armed forces, and joined Moscow University as a student of history. After graduation, I worked for some six months on a German-language newspaper and from then on until recently – it's only two years since I retired – I worked under the Academy of Sciences at the Institute of World Economics. But of course all this background, and in particular the younger years that I spent in Germany, Paris and so on, the years spent in the army, which acquainted me with the life of the common people, my historical education and my work at the Institute of World Economics, all this helps me understand the present-day developments.

Ali: When you were in your teens did you ever hear your father talking about Stalinism and what was going on in the country? After all, this was the period when an entire generation of old Bolsheviks was destroyed. Did your father ever discuss this with you, or was it a forbidden zone, which could be discussed silently in one's head, but never aloud?

Gershfeld: This is a difficult question. You see, my father firmly and clearly stated that all the reprisals against the old Bolsheviks in the army and in the diplomatic corps were a very dangerous thing and sheer lunacy. He said that, of course, at home, and I was absolutely ignorant of what he said or did not say at work. He was working in the realm of foreign relations. You should also remember that from the age of sixteen I spent most of my time away from home. Of course, I knew and my father never made it a secret for me that all these years my army career was very much hampered by all these things. In my character references, in my records, there was the reference to my uncle and to my father being expelled from the party, so I had a purely military career and never reached the top, general staff or anything like that. My father used to say that the victory of the Soviet Union in the Second World War was the victory of the Soviet people despite Stalinism. It is very difficult to go out and explain this to everyone. The victory of Soviet power despite

Stalin, that is very difficult to explain to common people.

Ali: Could you explain the transition from working in the Institute of World Economics to becoming part of the new, unofficial perestroika movement through the Federation of Socialist Clubs?

Gershfeld: My work at the Institute of World Economics was always uneasy for me, since I tend to stick to global views. In working out my globalist patterns I have always looked for positive solutions rather than confrontation, as far as the policy of the Soviet Union is concerned. The first clash I had at the Institute was on Sino-Soviet relations, and I had to my credit a number of writings on the issue. One, which has become a classic by now, was written in 1976 and called 'The Possibilities of War between China and the Soviet Union'. I was even fired from the Institute in 1967/68 for my position on China and reinstated only a year later. Although I was of the opinion that Maoism, which very much smelled of Stalinism, was very detrimental to China, I still held the Soviet Union responsible for the break-up of international relations. And in spite of my great respect for Nikita Khrushchev for his exposure of Stalinism, I believe that the break in Sino-Soviet relations was one of his most serious blunders, even a crime. You see, it was just a continuation of domestic policy where a lack of respect towards the human being inside the country or a lack of respect towards constituent republics within a country was extended to a foreign nation. Of course, the Soviet-American détente and the spirit of Camp David were quite correct. But he should have gone to Washington via Peking and thus represented the interests of the whole socialist community.

The next conflict was over Soviet-Czechoslovak relations. Objectively speaking, of course, the Soviet Union is the stronghold of the progressive forces worldwide and the driving force in the overall development of the socialist world. But in actual fact it proved to be one of the major counter-revolutionary forces, and I regard the invasion by Soviet troops of Czechoslovakia as an act of counter-revolution. It objectively merges with the counter-revolution in the West in 1968. The conservatives in the West were trying to submerge the revolution in the West, and we were trying to suppress the revolution in Eastern Europe. And thus we sort of suspended the whole revolutionary process in Europe.

Also, we are objectively to blame for the Polish events of 1980. If we had supported Czechoslovakia in 1968, the subsequent history of the whole of Europe, to say nothing of the development of revolutionary processes in Western Europe, would have been different. Of course this history goes back to Stalin's times, when

Hitler annihilated the German communists, but those who tried to find refuge here were killed by Stalin, and the Soviet invasion of Czechoslovakia also determined the relationship with China. The Chinese and Yugoslavs had every right to expect a Soviet invasion; it was a terrible distortion of Leninist foreign policy in the spirit of the traditional imperial politics of Tsarist Russia.

But such a policy is not in the interests of Russia. It was the international left-democratic movement that saved Russia in 1918 under the slogan, 'Hands off revolutionary Russia', and in the Second World War we fought against fascism in alliance with the world's democratic forces. In the post-war period, a great impact on the development of the two systems was made by the world revolutionary movement, with Third World revolutions preventing world imperialism from an onslaught on the Soviet Union, and then the war in Vietnam showing up the futility of US military power and providing the Soviet Union with an opportunity to achieve military parity.

I'm all for Gorbachev, but there still exists a tendency to underestimate the left-democratic forces and movements in our world. Too much emphasis is given to the relationships between the Tsars, the monarchs, and too little to the improvement of relationships between left-democratic and socialist movements. I can understand that Strauss is an important interlocutor, but on the other hand Lafontaine and the Green Party, the Labour movement, communists and all the other diversified left-progressive movements of the world are a more important factor.

Ali: What was the extent of your disagreements with the hierarchy at the Institute of World Economics? Was it exclusively political?

Gershfeld: Well, of course there was a constant friction on any issue connected with the Third or First World. I was studying at three levels, the first being the global questions, so I made an attempt to work out a global, overall strategy for the Soviet Union in terms of foreign policy. I must admit that so far we have not had that overall strategy. We are only beginning to shape it, not only in politics: but in other fields too – for example, production, consumer relations, transport – we do not yet have overall, global strategies.

As to the relationship of the Soviet Union with the developing and socialist countries, my field of interest was military strategy, and here again I had a very serious clash with my Institute. One of my manuscripts was called 'Peaceful Offensive'. But once again this title was treated rather shallowly and they regarded it as a catch-phrase. So my idea was of a political offensive, 360 degrees clockwise around the frontiers of the Soviet Union and globally. I must say that Gorbachev's addresses in the Far East, in Murmansk, and in Yugoslavia are to a certain extent in a correct direction, but my idea was of a global, all-round peaceful offensive. But at least what he is saying is part of that strategy. And, of course, I had clashes on the Afghanistan issue. When we first started to contemplate the idea of invading Afghanistan, they could hear my shouts all through the several storeys of the building, and not because I am a pacifist. I am an officer and a military man: if I were a young captain in the army I would be participating in the war in Afghanistan. My position was that it was a morally wrong, stupid and unproductive act. As the lawyers say, it was the abuse of the norms of necessary defence. Any kind of assistance – scientific, economic, military – was, of course, necessary, but invasion was a terrible mistake.

Ali: Why is someone of your obvious talents not in the CPSU?

Gershfeld: I am a member of the party.

Ali: So you're a member of the party and of the unofficial club?

Gershfeld: of course. One does not preclude the other. All my life I have taken the liberty of thinking and saying what I deem important and of course I have to pay for it.

Ali: And the discussion leading up to the June conference, will the party cell to which you belong let you participate and discuss policies?

Gershfeld: I'll try to do my best. I am doing it at every opportunity, and I maintain cooperation with a number of institutes, including the new institute on Western Europe. And another direction is my interview with you. This is also part of my global efforts.

Ali: The first time I came to your house I was very struck by two things – your amazing collection of books and the poster of Che Guevara. He was the one person whose portrait we carried in the sixties on the streets of Europe. What do you think of Che?

Gershfeld: I don't believe either in god or in heroes but the image of Christ as the image of the foremost personality is very moving and touching to me. And such personalities as Che Guevara are the revolutionary heroes who continued the line of serving the people to their last breath. I am a Bolshevik, and of course that is why he is my hero. The problem is not that he chose the wrong time and the wrong country where he was killed in the last battle. That was a tactical mistake, but his general line of serving the world progressive left-democratic movement, that is sacred. So he is one of the saints of our revolutionary . . .

Ali: I am very happy to hear you say this because in the sixties the Soviet press and the Eastern European official press were attacking him as an adventurist and nothing more.

Gershfeld: This can be explained unfortunately by the counter-revolution of the sixties in our country, when that son-of-a-bitch Yuri Zukov, a political analyst of *Pravda* whom I know, used the same words to describe the revolutionary students of Paris as devils and provocateurs.

Ali: What do you think of the chances of Gorbachev succeeding?

Gershfeld: Well, he has every chance of success, beyond any doubt. Another question is how complete that success will be. You see, Khrushchev launched his offensive at a time when the country was not prepared and he was supported only by Moscow and Leningrad. Now Gorbachev enjoys the support of vast masses because the country has changed.

Firstly, in terms of theory, the history of all social formations has passed through certain stages, starting from dictatorship, which testifies to the weakness of the formation: slavery in Rome, feudal Europe and present day capitalism. Secondly, the Soviet Union is a great socialist world power. We are one of the two superpowers of the world. On the basis of this force, of this strength, both internal and external changes occur. We are, of course, a young superpower and the misfortune of all these Brezhnevs and the other rubbish which is still in power is that they know that they belong to a superpower, but they don't realise it. If a demonstration of some refuseniks is being dispersed nowadays or if they invade Afghanistan, this is the inferiority complex which does not give them the freedom of spirit to realise that being a great superpower we can afford all sorts of demonstrations and all sorts of regimes in Afghanistan as well as a one-sided, major reduction of military forces.

On the experience of the great reductions in the armed forces realised by Khrushchev – over one million – one can state with full responsibility that it would be quite favourable for the Soviet Union to reduce its army unilaterally by 50% towards the year 2000. We must start to reduce our armaments and troops unilaterally, starting with the Pacific Ocean up to the Urals, say during three or four years, then to liquidate the China frontline leaving intact only the defence of the sea coast.

The policy of Gorbachev has undoubtedly borne great fruit already. Our next-door neighbours realise that we are a peaceful state or have become such. China has already reduced its army by one million and is working on the second million. Yugoslavia has reduced the term of military service, thus reducing the army, and Romania is cutting back on its military budget. These are our next-door neighbours, who were afraid of our interference after 1968.

And finally, my Gorbachev, whom I like very much, and Shevardnadze, who is also very much to my liking, are now saying that the German Question could be solved in a hundred years. For all these one hundred years I cannot agree and believe that the left and the left-democratic world movement must today change their vision of the unification of Germany, and not let the German Right monopolise it. It is quite understandable that the process of unification itself is at present seen as an obstacle to solving the problems between East and West, to the progress of disarmament, and that the prospect of German neutrality scares NATO and the Warsaw Pact. But we, the left-democratic movement of the world must raise this question and table it for consideration right now. We must work out our stand on it and in the global system of disarmament; we must also introduce this issue and fight for it. Only this can prevent the Third World War. For a neutral Scandinavia, Germany, Austria and Balkans will completely seize the space for conflict between the East and the West.

Ali: I just want to thank you because this has been one of the most stimulating interviews, and when we publish it in Western Europe people will be amazed that a rank-and-file member of the CPSU, moreover one who is a former colonel in the Red Army, thinks and talks like this.

Gershfeld: Unfortunately, as in technology, the gap between innovation and its implementation is very great. We must try to bring that time, the time of implementation, closer by our words and our deeds. Both in this country and in the whole world. It is my pleasure to have you here for this interview. I am looking forward to many more meetings like this and I am sure you will come again. I feel that spiritually we are akin. Same as all the left democrats. I also regard myself as a Bolshevik but in the tradition of the 1920s, and I sympathise with the Green Party, which to my mind is a very promising movement.

Ali: So you're really a Green Bolshevik!

Gershfeld: Who has anything against the colour green? You see, I am not only a theoretician – I am all for an ideal politics, and I believe that science must build up an ideal politics because the functionaries of the Ministry of Foreign Affairs will mar and spoil it, obviously . . .

So the Greens invited me on a lecture tour. I could not confirm it at that time because I am fat and lazy, but after taking counsel with my wife and friends I have decided to accept the invitation. I hope we meet again and I hope that the Soviet Union moves from a Dictatorship of Weakness to a Democracy of Strength.

Tariq Ali
(First published in *Labour Focus on Eastern Europe*)